ZULULAND
SAFARIS

CONSERVATION CORPORATION AFRICA
PHINDA ROCK LODGE

LESOTHO
SUN

Ezulwini Sun

SOFITEL HOTEL
SENEGAL

MALAWI PROTEA HOTELS

Dhow Palace
ZANZIBAR

A'ZAMBEZI
RIVER LODGE

VICTORIA FALLS
L★★★

SWAZI
TRAILS

LAM
MOZAMBIQUE

SOUTH AFRICAN
AIRWAYS·EXPRESS·AIRLINK

VENDA
SUN

AL·BAY TRAVEL SERVICES
A.B.T.S.

UBUNTU SAFARIS cc

LILAYI LODGE

COOKING FROM

CAPE
TO
CAIRO

A TASTE OF AFRICA

DORAH SITOLE AND

TRUE LOVE MAGAZINE

Tafelberg Publishers
28 Wale Street
Cape Town 8001

First published 1999

Publisher Dick Wilkins
Commissioning Editor Marga Collings
Editors Elizé Lübbe and Sean Fraser
Designer Mandy McKay
Proofreader Sylvia Grobbelaar
Indexer Elizé Lübbe
Production Manager Andrew de Kock

Reproduction by Unifoto (Pty) Ltd, Cape Town
Printed and bound by Tien Wah Press (Pte) Ltd, Singapore

ISBN 0-624-03817-3

PHOTOGRAPHIC CREDITS:

CameraPix: pp. 102, 103

Dorothy Schalkwyk: pp. 28 (bottom left), 32, 44, 45, 46,
49, 50, 51, 56, 57, 60, 81

Gerald Cubitt: pp. 36 (bottom left), 63, 69

Jacek Kropinsky: title page, pp. 3, 7 (top left), 8, 92,
94, 95, 97, 98, 99, 100, 101, 110, 111, 112, 113, 114,
115, 116, 117, 124, 125, 126, 127, 128, 129, 130, 131,
140 (centre top; right top), 141 (left top, centre and
bottom; centre bottom; right bottom), 142 (left top,
centre and bottom; centre bottom; right top and centre)

John Peacock: pp. 6, 7 (bottom right), 11, 15, 18, 19, 22,
25, 26, 27, 30 (bottom), 31, 33, 35, 39, 41, 43, 47, 48, 52, 53,
54, 55, 58, 59, 61, 64, 65, 66, 67, 68, 71, 72, 73, 74 (bottom
left), 76, 77, 79, 80, 82, 84, 85, 86, 87, 88, 89, 90, 91, 93, 96,
104, 105, 106, 106, 108, 109, 118, 119, 120, 121, 122, 123,
132, 133, 134, 135, 136, 137, 138, 139, 140 (left top, centre
and bottom; centre bottom; right top), 141 (centre top; right
top and centre), 142 (centre top; right bottom)

Mark Skinner: pp. 8, 9

Paul Gordon: pp. 10, 13, 14, 17

Roger de la Harpe: 20, 21, 28 (top right), 36 (top right),
62 (bottom left), 74 (top right), 75

True Love Magazine: pp. 4, 37, 83

Walter Knirr: 29, 62 (top right)

Food Stylist Dorah Sitole
Assistant on photoshoots Cordelia Molewe
Props courtesy of:
    The Crockery Warehouse
    Loads of Linen
    Indaba Curios

ACKNOWLEDGEMENTS:

Some South African traditional recipes are winning entries
from *True Love Magazine* readers' competition sponsored by
Fedics. The following chefs and cooks contributed recipes:

Botswana: Chef Frank Wiese, Miss Tash Sparrow and
    Mrs Sebautlwang 'Madinko' Tseko.

Egypt: Chef Faisal Abu Saada, Mrs Nadia Moursi and
    Mrs Jeannette Bedewi

Ghana: Chef Alex Asare and Mrs. Mercy Debrah

Kenya: Chef Gift Mwasho and Mama Omodi

KwaZulu-Natal: Chef Sipho Mathaba and
    Mrs Joyce Mbuyaze

Lesotho: Chef Manraz Rambocous and Mrs Olive Makenete

Malawi: Chef John Mafemula (Nkopolo Lodge) and
    Chef Richard Makawa (Mount Soche Hotel)

Morocco: Chef M'hamed Harbroune and
    Mrs Minah Abuane

Mozambique: Chef Orlando Lipanga and
    Mrs Joseffina Lenato Simbine

Senegal: Chef Arista Mandy and The Saint Germain
    Restaurant, Gore Island.

Swaziland: Chef Musa Mkhatshwa and
    Chef Dave Boyjoonauth

Transkei: Chef Emmanuel Dlamini, Mrs Mpumi Maqungo
    and Mrs Joyce Phoqela

Western Cape: Chef Ralph Cupido and Mrs Cass Abrahams

Venda: Vho Masindi Mudau

Zambia: Chefs Lee Wilson, Martin Chasunkwa and
    Nchonga Daka and Mrs Doreen Mwale.

Zanzibar: Chef Matloub Abdul, Chef Issa Khamis Mohamed,
    Mr Dipak Joshi and Miss Rabia Mwini

Zimbabwe: Chef Charles Musakaruka

OPPOSITE *Lobster Mayonnaise*

FOREWORD

Cooking from Cape to Cairo is not only 'A Taste of Africa' but an enriching, enlightening and empowering experience of our continent – qualities that *True Love Magazine*, South Africa's leading magazine for young, modern black women, aims to capture in all its features. For our Food Editor Dorah Sitole and photographer John Peacock, travelling through Africa was sometimes challenging, yet the visuals and information they brought back with them are a stunning testament to Africa's beauty, her diversity, her potential and her vibrant and dynamic personality. Through this book, *True Love Magazine* introduces the culture and cuisine of our continent in a manner that is positive, uplifting and confirms that the African Rennaisance should and can become a reality.

For Africans we hope *Cooking from Cape to Cairo* will not only revive your interest in African cuisine but also your dignity and pride in being African. And to the rest of the world we say: 'Enjoy the journey'.

Khanyi Dhlomo-Mkhize
Editor *True Love Magazine*
JUNE 1999

SPONSORS

The author, True Love Magazine and Tafelberg Publishers would like to thank the following sponsors who in many different ways made this book possible. Special thanks to Michelle Camps for organising all the travel arrangements.

South African Airways

South African Express Airways

South African Airlink

Al-Bay Travel Services (Senegal)

Air Malawi

A'Zambezi River Lodge (Zimbabwe)

The Cellars-Hohenort (Cape Town, South Africa)

Conservation Corporation Africa
      (Phinda Rock Lodge, KwaZulu-Natal, South Africa)

Ezulwini Sun (Swaziland)

Falcon Africa Safaris (Zanzibar and Ghana)

Gaborone Sun (Botswana)

Go Africa Tours (Mozambique)

Hotel Cardoso (Maputo, Mozambique)

Lesotho Sun

Lilayi Lodge (Zambia)

Malawi Protea Hotels

Marina Lodge (Richards Bay, KwaZulu-Natal, South Africa)

747 Travel (Egypt and Kenya)

Sofitel Hotel (Senegal)

Travel Vision (Zimbabwe)

Ubuntu Safaris (Zambia and Senegal)

Umtata Holiday Inn Garden Court
      (Eastern Cape, South Africa)

Venda Sun (South Africa)

The Zambian Safari Company

Zimbabwe Express Airlines

Dhow Palace (Zanzibar)

Egypt Air

Kenya Airways

LAM (Mozambique)

Metavia Airlines

Spier Wine Estate (Stellenbosch, South Africa)

Swazi Trails

Tourism Services Zimbabwe

Zululand Safaris

CONTENTS

INTRODUCTION

It has always been my wish to document the culinary experiences of my continent, Africa. What seemed to be an insurmountable task or a dream, happened sooner than I had anticipated.

In Zulu we say: *'Ukwanda kwaliwa umtha-kathi'* (only a witch will stand in the way of progress). This cookbook had to happen and only a magazine like True Love, that recognises the virtues of Africa and its people, could put it together. I had a short deliberation with the dynamic, and young but wise, editor of *True Love Magazine*, Khanyi Dhlomo-Mkhize, on how great it would be for *True Love Magazine*, as

BELOW *Beans, pulses and cereals on sale at a street market.*

the leading black women's magazine in the country, to publish a book on African cuisine. Not only did she become excited about the idea – she also made sure that it happened. With the assistance of the very capable Michelle Camps, trips to the various African countries were arranged, and my bags were packed and ready for the journey of my life. What excellent timing that this happened at the close of the century, and before first world civilisation and urbanisation erode our culinary heritage altogether.

It would give me great joy to see African food, in its entirety, on the centre stage of the worlds' cuisine. The few books written about African food, concentrate on West and North African cuisine. If anything is mentioned about South African cuisine, it is usually only about Afrikaans or Cape Malay food. Nothing wrong with that, but there is much more – South Africa has an array of exciting local foods, from villages and vibrant townships, through to the cities. What a pleasure it was to visit all these

ABOVE *Mint tea is a favourite after-dinner beverage.*

remote corners of our beautiful land and to get to grips with our wonderful food!

My wish is that this book will inspire everyone who reads it to become excited about Africa. Our cuisine is definitely the cuisine to watch out for in the new millennium. The food that has nourished our people for centuries, is an integral part of our lives. Granted, culture is not static, but we cannot allow the basic flavours that shaped our palates to be eradicated.

North Africa with its rich Arab-influenced cuisine, has undoubtedly made an impact on international food trends. West African food influences are seen as far as the USA, where Creole and Cajun gumbos celebrate the

versatility of African ingredients. East Africa's coconuts and the wonderful spices of Zanzibar have added an exotic touch to the gourmet foods of the world. The lakes of Central Africa are teeming with fish, an important source of income and a major part of the diet. The shores of this great continent also abound with a rich variety of seafood, so fish and seafood form an important part of African cuisine.

Through the pages of this book, Southern Africa will at last make its contribution to International cuisine. Its rich, nutritious and robust foods include dry beans, samp, maize-rice and maize-meal, cornrice, sorghum, groundnuts, offal, caterpillars, dried meat and vitamin-packed *morogo*, unusual root vegetables like *amadumbe* and the more exotic meats such as ostrich and zebra. These and many other foodstuffs have nurtured the people of this continent since ancient times.

The people of Africa willingly shared their culinary secrets with me. For this I am grateful. Compiling this book would have been very difficult were it not for the kind chefs, house-wives and caterers who hosted my photographers and me. I wish I had gone to each and every African country, but that would have taken a lifetime. I also wish I had documented each and every recipe from the countries I visited, but that would have filled several volumes. However, the

recipes in this book are the most popular and most of them are national dishes. They will definitely give you a taste of the culinary culture of our continent! Because not all the African ingredients are well known, I have included a photographic section for easy reference.

At last there is some record of food from Cape to Cairo for our children and generations to come. I know you will get excited with these dishes, your tastebuds will be challenged by the flavours of the African continent.

May Africa accept this cookbook as my humble contribution to the African Renaissance.

Dorah Sitole
JUNE 1999

BELOW *Succulent 'LM' prawns sizzling in the pan.*

CAPE MALAY
SOUTH AFRICA

The Western Cape Province, characterised by a succession of brilliantly coloured mountain ranges, is perhaps most famous for Cape Town's Table Mountain, and the spectacular flowering plants that grace the mountain slopes and the surrounding country-side. The best known member of this unique *fynbos* plant kingdom is the protea, among them the king protea, the country's floral emblem, which grows abundantly in the region.

The Cape, however, is also where many of the country's cultures meet and blend. It is here that the Muslim community, commonly referred to as the Cape Malays, has established itself. The Cape Malay people, largely descendants of slaves and exiled dissidents from the East who arrived in the early days of the colony, are a perfect blend of Africa and the East. The Dutch settlers, who arrived at the Cape in 1652, brought with them highly skilled slaves from the Indonesian Archipelago and, of course, Malaysia to build and secure the prosperity of their colony. To this day, the Cape's distinctive architecture attests to the skill and craftsmanship of these people. Through the years, they remained a distinct entity, held together by their Eastern heritage and staunch Muslim faith, and contributed in no small way to the development of the fledgling colony.

On their arrival the Dutch had encountered indigenous Khoisan people hunting, herding sheep, and gathering *veldkos* and, in some cases, living off the fruits of the sea. It was, however, the arrival of the Muslims that had the most influence on the local cuisine. The slaves and exiles introduced a variety of spices – obtained from trading vessels passing the Cape en route to Europe from the East – into the dishes prepared for their Dutch masters.

They skilfully blended the ingredients, and slowly exposed the mixture to moist heat while maintaining the essential goodness of each ingredient. This method of cooking has evolved over 300 years and has resulted in what is essentially known today as Cape Malay cuisine.

The Cape Malay community at the Cape has retained its love for food, and each dish is still enhanced with exotic spices from their far-off ancestral islands. Typical and much-favoured dishes include *bobotie*, chicken *masala*, *roti*, *denningvleis*, *breyani*, *bredies*, and *boeber*. The *bredies*, or stews, and curries are usually served with yellow rice with raisins, and *sambals*.

LEFT *A colourful Malay fruit and vegetable seller.*
ABOVE *Young Malay girls at a celebration feast.*
OPPOSITE *Spectacular Table Mountain at sundown.*

CHICKEN MASALA

Serves 6

1 kg (2½ lb) chicken pieces
10 ml (2 t) masala
5 ml (1 t) ground cumin
5 ml (1 t) ground coriander
5 ml (1 t) turmeric
15 ml (1 T) crushed garlic
15 ml (1 T) crushed fresh ginger
1 green chilli, finely chopped
salt and pepper to taste
30 ml (2 T) vegetable oil
80 ml (5 T) vegetable oil for basting
2 tomatoes, cut into wedges
1 lemon, cut into wedges

1 Trim the chicken pieces.
2 Mix together the spices, garlic, ginger, chilli, salt and pepper. Add the oil and mix to a paste. Rub the paste into the chicken and leave for 1 hour.
3 Place the chicken in a baking tray, baste with oil and roast at 180 °C (350 °F/gas 4) for 45 minutes or until the chicken is cooked.
4 Serve on a platter and garnish with tomato and lemon wedges. Serve with roti (see page 11) and yellow rice (see page 16).

ROTI

SERVES 8

360 g (12 oz)/750 ml (3 cups) flour

5 ml (1 t) salt

50 ml (3 T) vegetable oil

enough water to form a soft dough

250 g (9 oz)/250 ml (1 cup) soft butter/margarine

oil for frying

1 Mix the flour and salt in a large mixing bowl. Add oil and rub it in with the fingertips until the mixture resembles fine breadcrumbs.

2 Add water and mix to a fairly soft dough. Roll out on a floured surface to the size of a 23 x 32 cm (9 x 13 in) Swiss-roll tin.

3 Spread the dough with softened butter and roll it up like a Swiss roll. Cover with a tea towel and allow to rest for 30 minutes.

5 Break off pieces of dough and form into balls the size of a tennis ball.

6 Roll out each ball into a disc the size of a dinner plate. Fry in hot oil for 2 minutes on each side. Serve immediately with chicken masala (*see* page 10).

> Roti is a flat bread which is usually served with curries. Small pieces are torn off with the fingers and used to scoop up the meat and sauces.

MUTTON BREYANI

Serves 6–8

1,5 kg (3½ lb) mutton on the bone
250 ml (1 cup) oil
3 large onions, sliced
15 ml (1 T) crushed ginger
15 ml (1 T) crushed garlic
6 medium potatoes, cubed
5 ml (1 t) salt
500 g (18 oz)/625 ml (2½ cups) basmati rice
250 g (9 oz)/375 ml (1½ cups) brown lentils
6 hard-boiled eggs
100 g (4 oz)/100 ml (7 T) butter, melted
3 ml (½ t) saffron

MARINADE

3 sticks cinnamon
5 cardamom pods
2 green chillies
2 ml (½ t) turmeric
5 ml (1 t) red masala
30 ml (2 T) breyani masala
5 whole cloves
5 peppercorns
1 large tomato, diced
250 ml (1 cup) buttermilk

GARNISH

2 ml (½ t) saffron
30 ml (2 T) fresh coriander
2 hard-boiled eggs, halved

1 Wash the mutton and cut into cubes. Prepare the marinade and marinate meat for 2 hours.
2 Heat the oil, add the onions, ginger and garlic and sauté until brown. Add the marinated meat and cook for 30 minutes.
3 Season the potatoes with salt and fry until golden. Parboil the rice, then strain and rinse.
4 Place the lentils in hot water and cook until soft. Slice the boiled eggs in half.
5 Spoon rice into a large baking dish, followed by layers of potatoes, meat, eggs and lentils.
6 Repeat the layers, ending with a layer of rice mixed with butter and saffron. Cover with grease-proof paper and bake for 1 hour at 160 °C (325 °F/gas 3).
7 Garnish with saffron, coriander and eggs.

ONION SAMBAL

Makes ± 250 ml (1 cup)

2 large onions, sliced
60 ml (4 T) each coarse salt and brown vinegar
30 ml (2 T) smooth apricot jam
60 ml (4 T) chopped coriander leaves (dhania)

1 Place the onions in a bowl and sprinkle with the salt.
2 Gently rub the salt and onion together with the fingertips to remove all bitter onion juice.
3 Wash thoroughly in a sieve under cold running water to remove the salt. Return to the bowl.
4 Mix the vinegar and apricot jam, pour over the onions. Sprinkle with coriander leaves and serve with any bredie.

CARROT AND CHILLI SAMBAL

Makes ± 500 ml (2 cups)

4 carrots, peeled and grated
salt to taste
2 red chillies, chopped
2½ ml (½ t) sugar
15 ml (1 T) currants

1 Sprinkle a little salt over the carrots, leave for about 15 minutes and drain.
2 Add the remaining ingredients and chill until needed.

TOMATO BREDIE

Serves 4–6

2 large onions, sliced

2 ml (½ t) peppercorns

2 ml (½ t) ground cloves

125 ml (½ cup) water

25 ml (2 T) vegetable oil

2 sticks cinnamon

1 kg (2½ lb) mutton, cut into cubes

30 mm (1 in) piece fresh ginger, finely chopped

2 cardamom pods

1 kg (2½ lb) very ripe tomatoes, chopped, or

3 tins (3 x 410 g/3 x 14 oz) chopped tomatoes

1 green chilli, chopped

6 medium potatoes, peeled and halved

salt, freshly ground pepper and

sugar to taste

chopped parsley

1 Place the onions, peppercorns, cloves and water in a large saucepan and heat until boiling. Simmer until all the water has been absorbed.

2 Add the oil and cinnamon and braise until the onions are golden. Add the meat, ginger and cardamom pods and stir thoroughly.

3 Turn down the heat, cover the saucepan with a tightly fitting lid and simmer for 30 minutes.

4 Add the tomatoes and chilli. Close the lid and simmer for 20 minutes.

5 Add the potatoes, salt, freshly ground pepper and sugar. Replace the lid and simmer until the potatoes are cooked.

6 Garnish with chopped parsley and serve on a bed of yellow rice (*see* page 16).

Chicken may be used instead of mutton but then the cooking time must be reduced to 60 minutes.

DENNINGVLEIS

SERVES 8–10

3 large onions, sliced

25 ml (2 T) vegetable oil

5 plump garlic cloves, crushed

5 allspice

6 cloves

2 bay leaves

1 green chilli, finely chopped

10 ml (2 t) freshly ground black pepper

1 kg (2½ lb) mutton, cut into portions

25 ml (2 T) seedless tamarind

250 ml (1 cup) boiling water

5 ml (1 t) ground nutmeg

salt to taste

1 Heat the oil in a large saucepan, add the onions and fry until soft. Add the garlic, allspice, cloves, bay leaves, chilli and pepper.

2 Layer the meat on top of the onions. Close the saucepan with a tightly fitting lid and simmer for 30–40 minutes.

3 Soak the tamarind in boiling water. Allow to cool. Pour the tamarind through a sieve, pressing all the juices through with a spoon. Pour the tamarind liquid over the meat and sprinkle with nutmeg. Season to taste and simmer for 10–15 minutes. Serve with yellow rice (*see* page 16).

BOBOTIE

Serves 8

2 thick slices stale white bread

250–300 ml (1–1½ cups) water

15 ml (1 T) vegetable oil

50 g (2 oz)/50 ml (3 T) butter

2 large onions, chopped

800 g (1½ lb) beef mince

3 garlic cloves, crushed

15 ml (1 T) masala

5 ml (1 t) turmeric

10 ml (2 t) ground cumin

10 ml (2 t) ground coriander

3 whole cloves

2 ml (½ t) peppercorns

5 allspice

125 ml (½ cup) sultanas

60 ml (4 T) flaked almonds

5 ml (1 t) dried mixed herbs

25 ml (2 T) chutney

salt and freshly ground black pepper to taste

6–8 lemon leaves

250 ml (1 cup) milk

2 eggs, beaten

1 Soak the bread in water.

2 Fry the onions in the oil and butter until just transparent.

3 Place all the other ingredients, except the bread, lemon leaves, milk and egg, in a large bowl and mix.

4 Add the fried onions in their oil to the mixture. Squeeze the water from the bread, add to the meat and mix well.

5 Spread in a greased ovenproof dish. Roll the lemon leaves into spikes and insert into the mixture.

6 Bake at 180 °C (350 °F/gas 4) for 30 minutes. Lightly beat the eggs and milk together and pour over the meat. Bake until the egg mixture has set. Serve with yellow rice (*see* the recipe on this page).

> A lovely blend of flavours accounts for the popularity of this well-known Cape Malay dish. It used to be common practice among the Dutch and Malay communities, and to some extent still today, to serve yellow rice as part of a meal after a funeral. The method of colouring rice with turmeric was introduced by the Indian immigrants. For yellow rice without the raisins, step 3 in the recipe is left out.

YELLOW RICE WITH RAISINS

SERVES 6

1 litre (4 cups) water

500 ml (2 cups) uncooked white rice

10 ml (2 t) turmeric

2 sticks cinnamon

3 cardamom pods

salt and sugar to taste

175 ml (¾ cup) seedless raisins or sultanas

30 g (1 oz)/30 ml (2 T) butter

1 Heat the water in a saucepan until it boils. Add the rice, turmeric, cinnamon, cardamom pods, salt and sugar. Turn down the heat, cover and simmer gently for 20 minutes or until the rice is cooked through and all the liquid has been absorbed.

2 Pour the rice into a colander and rinse under running water to remove excess turmeric. Return to the saucepan.

3 Add the raisins or sultanas, mix in lightly and steam gently for a further 15 minutes.

4 Add the butter and fluff the rice with a fork. Serve warm with masalas or bobotie.

WATERBLOMMETJIE-BREDIE

SERVES 6

125 ml (½ cup) water

500 g (18 oz) *waterblommetjies*, trimmed
and well washed

1 potato, sliced

1 onion, sliced

1 garlic clove, crushed

salt and freshly ground black pepper to taste

5 ml (1 t) lemon juice, optional

15 ml (1 T) chopped sorrel

1 Let the water boil, then add *waterblommetjies*,
potato, onion, garlic and seasoning. Simmer for
35 minutes or until tender but still crisp.
2 Add the sorrel and lemon juice, heat through.
Serve the stew on rice.

> *Waterblommetjies* or Cape pondweed
> (*Aponogeton distachyos*) grow in the dams and
> vleis of the Cape. These add body and flavour to
> soups and stews. Before cooking, cut off the
> stems and soak the flowers overnight in
> salted water to cleanse.

BOEBER

35 g (1 oz)/45 ml (3 T) sago

125 ml (½ cup) water

50 g (2 oz)/50 ml (3 T) butter

150 g (5 oz)/250 ml (1 cup) fine vermicelli,
broken into small pieces

8–10 cardamom pods

3 cinnamon sticks of about 2,5 cm (1 in) each

200 g (7 oz)/325 ml (1½ cups) sultanas

2 litres (3½ pints/8 cups) milk

400 g (14 oz)/500 ml (2 cups) sugar

a few drops of rose water to flavour (optional)

1 Soak the sago in the water for 30 minutes.

2 Melt butter in a saucepan and gently brown
the vermicelli in the butter, stirring constantly
to prevent it from sticking. Add the rest of the
ingredients, except the rose water.

3 Simmer, stirring occasionally until thick and
creamy. Add rose water to taste. Serve hot or cold.
VARIATION: Grated unsalted nuts and coconut
may be added to vary the flavour of the *boeber*.

On the fifteenth night of Ramadan, the Muslim
holy month, this thick, spicy milk pudding is
served to celebrate the middle of the fast. More
sago may be added for a thicker consistency.

XHOSA
SOUTH AFRICA

The Eastern Cape Province, traditional home of the Xhosa people, stretches from the foot of the Drakensberg range through undulating hills and lush valleys toward the Wild Coast, and is infamous for its many tortuous roads that wind around rocky headlands and end abruptly in cliffs. The untamed wilderness of the Wild Coast boasts magnificent natural features, such as the Hole-in-the-Wall, the Waterfall Bluff and vast rocky reefs that extend far out to sea.

Traditionally, the Xhosa lived in homesteads where the members were all related to the head of the clan. Today, most still reside in the Cape, with a greater concentration of *ezilalini* (villages) along the eastern coastal strip, in the former homelands of Transkei and Ciskei. The Eastern Cape is predominantly rural and the traditional homesteads of the Xhosa still lay scattered over the veld here. Many remain true to their cultural heritage: women tend to the home and lands, while the menfolk earn the family's keep.

The Xhosa are divided into a number of large clans, including the Thembu, Bomvana, Mpondo and others, and their lively native tongue is characterised by clicking sounds. Like most other African peoples, the Xhosa traditionally wore skin garments. Later, they used blankets dyed with a particular type of red soil, hence the term 'the red blanket people'. Women wore large turbans, beads, copper bracelets and braided skirts, while a long pipe was a status symbol of a mature married woman. Many women in the rural areas still wear the traditional apparel, but in the cities these are worn only occasionally or for celebrations.

Maize – whole, dried, crushed or ground – is a staple food in most of Africa, but it is the Xhosa who must surely be the custodians of this versatile grain. Although they contributed samp and beans to South Africa's cuisine, their influence has extended far beyond that of samp. Their popular soup, *isopho*, is a combination of beans and corn, and *ugadugadu* is a tasty blend of dried pumpkin and maize-meal. *Umqa* is fresh pumpkin mashed with corn. *Amarhewu*, *imbila*, *umvubo* – you name it, it is certain to contain some form of maize.

LEFT *A young Xhosa man wearing typical beadwork.*
ABOVE *Xhosa women in traditional dress.*
OPPOSITE *A Xhosa village in the Eastern Cape.*

INYAMA YEGUSHA

MUTTON CASSEROLE

SERVES 4

60 ml (4 T) oil

1 kg (2½ lb) mutton, cut into pieces

4 medium onions, chopped

500 g (18 oz) carrots, sliced

2 large tomatoes, chopped

salt and pepper to taste

60 g (2½ oz)/125 ml (½ cup) flour

1 Heat the oil and brown the meat.

2 Add onions, carrots, tomatoes and seasoning.

3 Simmer gently for 45 minutes or until the meat is cooked and tender.

4 Mix flour and a little water to a paste and add to meat. Simmer until thickened. Serve with samp and beans (*see* the recipe for *umngqusho,* page 24).

ULUSU LWENKOMO

STEWED OX TRIPE

SERVES 4–6

1 kg (2½ lb) stomach

1 kg (2½ lb) intestines

water

salt and pepper to taste

1 Clean the stomach and intestines thoroughly and rinse under cold running water.

2 Place in a saucepan and cover with salted water. Heat until boiling, reduce the heat and simmer gently for 3 hours or until very soft. Serve with *pap* (porridge) or dumpling.

UMQA

PUMPKIN AND CORN

SERVES 4

2 kg (4½ lb) pumpkin

125 ml (½ cup) water

5 ml (1 t) salt

sugar to taste

1 kg (2½ lb)/4 x 250 ml (4 cups) whole kernel corn, cooked and off the cob

250 ml (1 cup) water

1 Peel and dice the pumpkin. Place pumpkin in a saucepan and add the water and salt.

2 Cook gently for about 15 minutes until the pumpkin is soft. Add sugar.

3 Stir in the corn and simmer gently for another 15 minutes.

INYAMA YENKUKHU

CHICKEN CASSEROLE

Serves 4–6

1 whole chicken of 750 g–1 kg (1½ lb–2½ lb)

60 ml (4 T) oil

4 medium onions, chopped

2 large tomatoes, chopped

salt and pepper to taste

75 ml (5 T) flour

1 Cut the chicken into pieces.

2 Heat the oil and fry the chicken until golden-brown.

3 Add the onions and cook for 5 minutes.

4 Add the tomatoes and seasoning, and simmer gently for 45 minutes or until cooked through.

5 Thicken the casserole with the flour, mixed with a little cold water.

> This dish is traditionally made using *umleqwa*, or chicken slaughtered at home.

ISOPHO

MAIZE AND BEAN SOUP

SERVES 4

500 ml (2 cups) fresh maize, cut from the cob

250 ml (1 cup) dried sugar beans,
soaked overnight

500 ml (2 cups) water

15 ml (1 T) oil

1 onion, chopped

5 ml (1 t) curry powder

1 potato, diced

salt to taste

1 Cook the maize and dried beans in the water until tender.

2 Heat the oil and fry the onion, curry powder and potatoes.

3 Add the onion and potatoes to the maize soup and simmer for about 1 hour, or until cooked. Serve hot.

INKUKHU NEMBOTYI

CHICKEN STRIPS WITH GREEN BEANS

SERVES 4–6

450 ml (2 cups) oil

1 onion, sliced

3 chicken breasts, deboned and cut into strips

salt to taste

5 ml (1 t) mixed masala, such as ginger and
garlic masala

250 ml (1 cup) green beans

250 ml (1 cup) chicken stock

1 Heat the oil and fry the onion until golden-brown. Add the chicken strips and continue to fry until soft. Sprinkle with salt and spices.

2 Wash and trim the green beans, but keep them whole. Add the beans and the stock to the chicken, and simmer gently until cooked through. Season with salt.

3 TO SERVE: Gently mix into cooked samp and beans (*see* the recipe for *umngqusho*, this page), or pile on top.

UMNGQUSHO

SAMP AND BEANS

SERVES 4–6

600 g (1½ lb)/750 ml (3 cups) samp
and beans

water

salt to taste

1 Soak the samp and beans overnight.

2 Rinse the samp and beans and place it in a saucepan. Pour in fresh water to cover, add salt and heat until boiling.

3 Simmer until tender, adding water whenever the samp and beans get dry. Cooking time is about 2 hours.

> Samp is made from maize kernels that have been stamped and broken but not ground as fine as maize-rice or maize-meal. Ready-mixed packets of samp and sugar beans can be bought from supermarkets. If these are not available, you can mix samp and sugar beans in equal quantities.

OPPOSITE, CLOCKWISE FROM RIGHT TO LEFT

Maize and Bean Soup, Chicken Strips with Green Beans

IMBILA

SOUR PORRIDGE

SERVES 4

240 g (9 oz)/500 ml (2 cups) maize-meal

120 g (4½ oz)/250 ml (1 cup) sorghum

1 litre (4 cups) water

1 Soak the maize-meal and sorghum overnight in the water. Retain the water.

2 Cook the mixture in the water in which it soaked for 20–30 minutes, stirring constantly. The porridge must be very runny; add boiling water if it thickens too much.

3 Allow the porridge to cool and let it rest for 4 hours so that the fermentation process can take place. Add sugar to taste before drinking. VARIATION: To make *amarhewu*, replace the sorghum with white maize-meal.

MAIZE WITH UMFINO

SERVES 4–6

1 medium cabbage, shredded

1 bunch spinach, shredded

1 bunch turnips, peeled and diced

1 bunch spring onions, chopped

170 g (6 oz)/250 ml (1 cup) maize-rice

180 g (6 oz)/375 ml (1½ cups) maize-meal

500 ml (2 cups) water

125 g (4½ oz)/125 ml (½ cup) butter/margarine

salt and pepper to taste

1 Wash and rinse the vegetables.

2 In a large saucepan, let the water boil and then add all the vegetables. Toss with a fork to mix and simmer for 10 minutes.

3 Add the maize-rice, mix through and then stir in the maize-meal. Use a wooden spoon to mix the ingredients to a pulp.

4 Cook over a low heat for 25 minutes, stirring occasionally.

5 Serve with meat dishes.

MAIZE-MEAL DUMPLING WITH VEGETABLES

SERVES 4

250 ml (1 cup) each milk and water

4 eggs

1 tin (410 g/14 oz) mixed vegetables, drained

50 g (2 oz)/75 ml (5 T) sugar

240 g (9 oz)/500 ml (2 cups) cake flour

120 g (4 oz)/250 ml (1 cup) maize-meal

10 ml (2 t) baking powder

boiling water

1 Beat together the milk, water and eggs. Add the vegetables.

2 Sift the dry ingredients together and add to the vegetable mixture.

3 Mix to a smooth, soft dough. Pour into a large greased enamel dish. Place the enamel dish in a saucepan about ⅓ full of boiling water.

5 Steam gently for about 1 hour or until the dumpling is cooked. Add more water to the saucepan if it dries out during cooking. Serve with meat and gravy.

INTLANZI WITH CABBAGE AND TOMATO RELISH

SERVES 4

1 whole maasbanker (intlanzi) or any other
firm white fish

60 g (2½ oz)/125 ml (½ cup) flour

salt and pepper to taste

60 ml (4 T) oil

50 g (2 oz)/50 ml (3 T) butter/margarine

500 ml (2 cups) cabbage, shredded

TOMATO RELISH

30 ml (2 T) oil

1 onion, chopped

1 medium tomato, chopped

3 ml (½ t) cayenne pepper

1 Gut and clean the maasbanker. Coat the fish
well with seasoned flour.

2 Heat the oil in a frying pan. Fry the fish on
both sides until nicely browned and cooked.

3 Tomato relish: Fry the onion, tomato and
cayenne pepper in a little oil in a separate pan.

4 Meanwhile, braise the shredded cabbage in
butter/margarine until soft.

5 Serve the fish whole on a bed of braised
cabbage, samp and beans (*see* the recipe for
umngqusho, page 24). Top with the tomato relish.

ZULU
SOUTH AFRICA

KwaZulu-Natal is the traditional home of the Zulu nation, the largest ethnic group in South Africa. The province itself is characterised by rolling hills that stretch out to the mighty *izintaba zokhahlamba* – the Drakensberg, or Barrier of Spears – and includes outstanding inland and marine nature reserves.

The origins of the Zulu nation can be traced to the late 1600s – since then the realm has had 15 rulers, including the present Zulu king, Zwelithini. Perhaps the best known of the warrior kings is Shaka, who set out to make the Zulu nation the most powerful and most feared on the southern African subcontinent. Like all of South Africa's tribes, the majority of Zulu have become

urbanised, but traditional customs are still upheld in the rural areas. *Isisu somhambi asingakanani, singang 'enso yenyonini* (a visitor's stomach is as small as the kidney of a bird), therefore, there is never too little food to feed strangers. Visitors to a traditional Zulu home are always offered food, and it is considered impolite to refuse.

Zulu cuisine is simple, and the women must be creative with the limited selection: maize-meal, sorghum, sweet potatoes, potatoes, *amadumbe* (similar to sweet potato, but with a coarse skin), melons and pumpkin are the most common ingredients. *Phutu* (crumbled porridge) is served with *amasi* (curdled milk) or tomato relish. Maize is often boiled or roasted on the cob, and women are often seen on sidewalks roasting corn on braziers and selling it to passers-by. Zulu men's favourite food is *inyama eyosiwe*, meat (chuck, steak or brisket) grilled over an open fire until it is cooked through and tender. This is served with *pap* (porridge) or samp, and is followed by a sip of sorghum beer, *umqombothi*. Zulu beer is highly intoxicating and is served only to adults. *Amarhewu*, a lighter drink of fermented maize-meal, is served to women and children.

The cultural heritage of KwaZulu-Natal also includes the legacy of settlers from India, whose descendants have become part of the essence of the region. Today, their legacy lives on not only in the Indian communities concentrated largely in and around Pietermaritzburg and Durban, but also in the contribution they have made to local cuisine – the exotic tastes, flavours and aroma of Eastern delights for which the cities – and, indeed, the province – is so well known.

LEFT *Zulu maidens dancing.*
ABOVE *A married Zulu woman displays her* isicholo *(head dress).*
OPPOSITE *The scenic Valley of a Thousand Hills, Zululand.*

RABBIT STEW WITH VEGETABLES

SERVES 6

1 rabbit of approximately 1,5 kg (3½ lb)

30 ml (2 T) cooking oil

1 onion, diced

3 potatoes, quartered

3 carrots, sliced

250 ml (1 cup) sliced green beans

250 ml (1 cup) water

salt and pepper

1 Cut the rabbit into portions. Heat the oil in a large pot and brown the rabbit pieces.
2 Add the onion to the pot and fry with the rabbit pieces until the onion is brown. Layer the potatoes, carrots and green beans on the meat. Add the water and seasoning.
3 Cover and simmer over a low heat for 1–2 hours until the meat is tender. Serve with beetroot leaf stew and *phutu* (*see* this page).

OPPOSITE, CLOCKWISE FROM TOP

Rabbit Stew, Phutu and Umbido

THREE-LEGGED POTS
The traditional three-legged cast-iron pot has been in use since the Dark Ages. It is thought that it was introduced into Africa through European traders. Today it is used all over the world. In South Africa it has become a traditional way of cooking for most feasts or celebrations. *Potjiekos* or one pot cooking has become a popular way of outdoor entertaining. Cooking over an open fire adds a unique flavour to the food. An added bonus is that the pot retains an even heat, which ensures that the food cooks slowly, at the same time conserving energy.

UMBIDO

BEETROOT LEAF STEW

SERVES 4–6

30 ml (2 T) oil

1 onion, finely chopped

500 g (18 oz) beetroot leaves

3 tomatoes, peeled and diced

salt and pepper

4 hard-boiled eggs, chopped

1 Heat the oil, add the onions and fry gently until transparent.
2 Add the beetroot leaves, tomatoes and seasoning. Simmer gently for 10 minutes until soft. Stir occasionally with a fork.
3 Carefully mix in the hard-boiled eggs. Serve on *phutu* (*see* the recipe below).

PHUTU

SERVES 4–6

250 ml (1 cup) water

360 g (12 oz)/750 ml (3 cups) maize-meal

1 Bring the water to the boil. Add maize-meal all at once without stirring, reduce heat and simmer about 20 minutes until cooked through.
2 Stir with a large fork until crumbly.

IPHALISHI LOBHONTSHISI

BUTTER BEAN PORRIDGE

SERVES 4

400 g (14 oz)/500 ml (2 cups) butter beans

water

salt and pepper to taste

60 ml (4 T) oil

1 medium onion, grated

2 garlic cloves, crushed

2 tomatoes, chopped

2 beef stock cubes, dissolved in:

650 ml (2½ cups) water

240 g (9 oz)/500 ml (2 cups) maize-meal

1 Cover the beans with water and soak overnight. Retain the water.

2 Bring beans and water to the boil. Season and cook until soft, then mash to a smooth paste.

3 Fry the onion and garlic in oil until soft. Add the tomatoes, beans and stock. Heat until boiling, add the maize-meal and mix well.

4 Cook for 35 minutes over medium heat, stirring occasionally. Serve hot with any relish.

ABOVE *Zulu basketwork and pottery.*

OPPOSITE, CLOCKWISE FROM TOP

Tomato and Onion Relish, Sour Milk Porridge, Butter Bean Porridge and Pumpkin Porridge.

IPHALISHI ELIMUNCU

SOUR MILK PORRIDGE

SERVES 4

500 ml (2 cups) sour milk

water

120 g (4½ oz)/250 ml (1 cup) maize-meal

125 ml (½ cup) water

1 Boil the sour milk and water. Add the maize-meal, stir and cook for 30–35 minutes.

2 Serve hot with tomato and onion relish.

ISIJEZA

PUMPKIN PORRIDGE

SERVES 4

10 pumpkin slices, peeled

salt and sugar or cinnamon sugar to taste

120 g (4½ oz)/250 ml (1 cup) maize-meal

250 ml (1 cup) cold water

500 ml (2 cups) hot water

1 Chop the pumpkin slices into small pieces. Sprinkle with salt and sugar. Add the cold water and cook until soft.

2 Mash the pumpkin and add the hot water. Let it boil and then add the maize-meal. Stir until well mixed.

3 Cook for 30 minutes over medium heat. Serve hot or cold with relish.

UMHLUZI WETAMATISI NE ANYANISI

TOMATO AND ONION RELISH

SERVES 4

45 ml (3 T) oil

3 onions, finely chopped

2 garlic cloves, crushed

6 large tomatoes, peeled and grated

5 ml (1 t) cayenne pepper

2 green or red chillies, seeded and chopped

salt and pepper to taste

1 Heat the oil, add the onions and garlic and sauté until transparent.

2 Add the tomatoes and all the remaining ingredients and cook through until the sauce is thick. Serve over *phutu*.

STIR-FRIED VEGETABLES WITH SWEET POTATO CRISPS

SERVES 2

45 g (1½ oz)/45 ml (3 T) butter

2–3 leeks, cut into long strips

1 large onion, sliced

½ cabbage, finely shredded

250 g (9 oz) spinach, washed and chopped

50 g (2 oz)/125ml (½ cup) sunflower seeds

salt and pepper to taste

CRISPS

3 sweet potatoes, peeled and thinly sliced

750 ml (3 cups) oil

5 ml (1 t) cumin

10 ml (2 t) sea salt

1 Melt the butter, add the leeks, onion and cabbage and cook until the vegetables are soft.

2 Add the spinach and sunflower seeds, stir to coat with butter. Season.

3 CRISPS: Heat the oil, add the sweet potatoes and fry until golden. Drain on brown paper or paper towels. Lightly sprinkle the sweet potatoes with cumin and sea salt. Serve the vegetables in the middle of a large platter and arrange the crisps around it.

SAMP PAELLA

SERVES 2

100 g (4 oz)/125 ml (½ cup) samp

1 litre water

45 g (1½ oz) 45 ml (3 T) butter

1 onion, chopped

4 mushrooms, finely chopped

1 green pepper, diced

125 ml (½ cup) white wine

3 mussels

45 ml (3 T) oil

6 prawns, peeled and cleaned

100 g (4 oz) kingklip, diced

4–6 cherry tomatoes

1 Cook samp in water until soft – do not stir, as stirring will make it mushy. Rinse and set aside.

2 Melt butter, add onion and mushrooms and sauté. Add the green pepper and sauté until soft.

3 In a separate saucepan, heat the wine until it boils and add the mussels. Simmer for 1 minute.

4 Heat the oil, add prawns and kingklip and fry.

5 Add the onion mixture to the fish. Add the samp, stir lightly and add the tomatoes. Spoon on a serving plate and top with the mussels.

6 VARIATION: Set mussels, tomatoes and prawns aside. Place samp in a mould and leave 15 minutes. Turn out on a heated serving platter and garnish with the mussels, tomatoes and prawns.

MAIZE-MEAL CUSTARD WITH CHOCOLATE SAUCE

SERVES 5

500 ml (2 cups) cream

10 ml (2 t) cinnamon

62,5 ml (½ cup) sugar

2 ml (½ t) vanilla essence

5 prunes, stoned

180 g (6 oz)/375 ml (1½ cups) maize-meal

250 ml (1 cup) milk

TOPPING

200 g (7 oz) dark chocolate

200 ml (1 cup) cream

1 Heat together the cream, cinnamon, sugar and vanilla essence.

2 Mix the maize-meal with the milk and add to the warm cream. Cook until thick.

3 Place the prunes in the base of a mould and pour maize-meal mixture on top. Cool to set.

4 TOPPING: Mix chocolate and cream, and melt in a double boiler. Turn mould out on a serving platter and pour sauce over just before serving.

OPPOSITE, CLOCKWISE FROM TOP

Stir-fried Vegetables, Maize-meal Custard with Chocolate Sauce, and Samp Paella

LESOTHO

From time immemorial the image of Lesotho is the smoke seeping through the thatch roofs of village huts, the smell of cow-dung fires, early morning sunlight bathing herd-boys as they scatter across the hills, the hooves of horses, and the greetings of blanket-clad men: *'Khotso, pula, nala'* ('Peace, rain and plenty').

Three quarters of Lesotho is dominated by the rugged and scantily populated Maluti mountains. Most of its 1.5 million population live in the low-land areas, and only a small percentage – around 5 per cent – live in and around the capital, Maseru. The country is completely surrounded by South Africa, and its economy and politics is thus much influenced by its larger neighbour.

The Basotho nation was created in the 19th century through the leadership of the dynamic military and diplomatic strategist, Moshoeshoe I, who forged together small chiefdoms, which had been torn apart by the destructive Difaqane wars of the Zulu king, Shaka. Basotholand merged with the Cape Colony until it was finally recognised as an independent kingdom in 1966. Today, the Basotho people are led by King Letsie III, a direct descendant of Moshoeshoe.

Rural folk still tend to wear the colourful and symbolically patterned blankets for which they are so well known, and the men don conical hats of straw, while the women are expert weavers. The Basotho are also known as *majapere*, 'the people who eat horse meat' – horses are plentiful, and are used for daily transport in this mountainous region – but this is not common practice. Horse meat is only eaten if a horse is killed accidentally, not if it dies of disease, and horses are never slaughtered for their meat.

The Basotho style of cooking is basic but nutritious. The family eats only home-grown vegetables and hand-raised chicken, and any-thing left over from the harvest is sun dried to make *mangangajane*. A nutritious meal could consist of *pap* (maize-meal porridge), steamed pumpkin with cinnamon, spinach stewed in beef stock, and stewed oxtail, a Basotho favourite, which is traditionally stewed in salted water until the meat falls off the bone. Beetroot salad is also very popular, and a meal may be considered incomplete without it. The beetroot is cooked, grated and then mixed with chopped onion, sugar and vinegar. The leaves make a very healthy and tasty side dish, cooked on their own or mixed with tomato and onion as *morogo*.

LEFT   *Basotho horseman riding through the mountains.*
ABOVE   *Basotho woman straining beer into a clay pot.*
OPPOSITE   *Typical mountainous Lesotho scenery.*

GINGER BEER

MAKES 2 LITRES (3½ PINTS)

5 ml (1 t) sugar

500 ml (2 cups) lukewarm water.

1 packet (10 g) brewer's yeast

30 ml (2 T) ground ginger

10 ml (2 t) tartaric acid

1 orange, sliced, or ½ pineapple, sliced

125 ml (½ cup) warm water

1 Dissolve the sugar in lukewarm water. Sprinkle with brewer's yeast and set aside for 10 minutes.

2 Mix together the ground ginger, tartaric acid and a tablespoon of lukewarm water and stir well.

3 Add the orange or pineapple slices.

4 Add the warm water, cover with a damp cloth and leave for 12 hours.

5 Strain the mixture and leave it in a cool place for 3 days before serving.

VARIATION: To make larger quantities, the ingredients may be increased proportionately. Ginger beer is a traditional drink and is always served at celebrations and feasts.

TING

SOUR PORRIDGE

SERVES 4

120 g (4½ oz)/250 ml (1 cup) maize-meal

250 ml (1 cup) maize-rice

375 ml (1½ cups) water

1 Mix all the ingredients in a plastic bowl.

2 Leave to stand for 2–3 days. Taste to see if the mixture is sour. If not, leave it for another day to ferment.

3 When the mixture is ready, pour 750 ml (3 cups) water in a saucepan and heat to boiling point.

4 Gradually add the fermented mixture, stirring continuously to eliminate lumps. Cover and simmer for 30 minutes or until cooked. Serve with liver and morogo (*see* this page and pages 42 and 64).

> Maize-rice, a rice-shaped grain made from maize, is sometimes mixed into sour porridge (*ting*). Maize-rice is available from most supermarkets. Corn-rice is a type of crushed wheat. The grains are larger than maize-rice and are round.

SEBETE SE HALIKILOENG WITH MOROGO

FRIED LIVER WITH MOROGO

SERVES 4

MOROGO

500 g (18 oz) dry morogo (thepe)

30 ml (2 T) water

salt and pepper

90 ml (6 T) milk

30 g (1 oz)/30 ml (2 T) butter/margarine

LIVER

500 g (18 oz) liver, cut into pieces

60 ml (4 T) oil

1 MOROGO: Wash the vegetables thoroughly, rinse and place in a saucepan. Add the water, salt and pepper. Cover and cook until the liquid is reduced. Add the milk and butter/margarine. Simmer until all the liquid is absorbed.

2 LIVER: Prick the liver with a fork and sprinkle it with salt. Fry in hot oil on both sides for 10–15 minutes.

3 Place the liver on the morogo. Serve with sour porridge (*see* this page).

OPPOSITE *Fried Liver with Morogo and Ting*

LEKHOTLOANE

POUNDED MEAT

SERVES 4–6

750 g–1 kg (1½–2½ lb) leg of lamb

1 litre (4 cups) water

45 ml (3 T) oil

2 onions, finely chopped

1 beef stock cube dissolved in:

250 ml (1 cup) hot water

salt and pepper to taste

1 Boil the leg of lamb in the water until soft and falling off the bone.

2 Cut the meat into portions and pound it until it resembles stringy mince.

3 Heat the oil and sauté the onions until transparent. Add the pounded meat and stock.

4 Simmer gently until the sauce thickens. Season and serve with steamed dumpling (*see* the recipe for *leqebekoane* on page 42) and *morogo* (*see* pages 38, 42 and 64) or spinach.

Steamed dumpling is popular among all African tribes and each one has a special way of making it. *Leqebekoane* is made with fermented maize-meal paste to give it a musty taste. The paste is prepared by mixing maize-meal with water and leaving it for at least two days to ferment. This dumpling is always steamed separately in a basin, never over a stew.

LIKAHARE

MIXED OFFAL

SERVES 4–6

1 kg (2½ lb) mixed offal (tripe, intestines, lungs, etc.)

2 vegetable stock cubes, dissolved in:

500 ml (2 cups) hot water

2 onions, sliced

salt and pepper to taste

1 Clean the offal thoroughly and rinse under cold running water.

2 Heat the stock to boiling point and add the meat. Cook gently for about 2 hours or until the meat is tender.

3 Remove meat from the sauce and slice thinly.

4 Add the onions to the sauce, return the meat, season and simmer for a further 30 minutes.

5 Serve warm on *nyekoe* (*see* the next recipe), with *morogo* (*see* pages 38, 42 and 64) or spinach.

NYEKOE

CORN RICE AND BEANS

SERVES 4–6

200 g (7 oz)/250 ml (1 cup) dry sugar beans

500 ml (2 cups) water

340 g (12 oz)/500 ml (2 cups) corn rice

60 g (2½ oz)/60 ml (4 T) butter/margarine

salt and pepper to taste

1 Place the sugar beans in a bowl and cover completely with water. Soak overnight. Drain.

2 In a saucepan, heat the water until it boils, add the beans and cook for 1 hour.

3 Add the corn rice, top up with water if necessary and cook gently for a further 1 hour.

4 Stir in the butter/margarine and season with salt and pepper to taste.

LEFT *Morogo is made from a variety of wild leaves.*

OPPOSITE *Mixed Offal, and Corn Rice and Beans.*

LEQEBEKOANE

STEAMED DUMPLING

SERVES 4–6

360 g (12 oz)/(750 ml (3 cups) flour
120 g (4½ oz)/250 ml (1 cup) fermented
maize-meal paste
1 packet (10 g) dry yeast
30 ml (2T) sugar
5 ml (1 t) salt
1 egg, beaten
± 500 ml (2 cups) lukewarm water, or
water mixed with milk

1 Sift the flour and mix in the dry ingredients.
2 Mix the egg with water. Add enough luke-warm water to the dry ingredients to form a soft and pliable dough. Knead for 10 minutes.
3 Cover the dough with plastic and leave to rise until doubled in size. Knock the dough down and place it in a greased enamel bowl. Allow to rise again until double in size before steaming.
4 Meanwhile, heat the water until it boils in a pot large enough to hold the bowl containing the dumpling. Immerse it in the hot water (the water should come ⅓ of the way up the sides of the dish). Seal the pot tightly and simmer gently for 1 hour. Try to avoid opening the saucepan during steaming. Replenish water if necessary.
5 TO SERVE: Cut the dumpling into wedges.

SECHU SA KHOHO

CHICKEN STEW

SERVES 4–6

1 whole chicken of 750g–1 kg (1½–2½ lb)
60 ml (4 T) oil
2 onions, chopped
1 clove garlic, crushed
3 medium tomatoes, peeled and chopped
2 chillies, seeded and chopped
1 chicken stock cube, dissolved in:
250 ml (1 cup) water
salt and pepper to taste

1 Cut the chicken into portions. Heat the oil and fry the chicken on all sides until brown.
2 Add the onions and garlic, and sauté until the onion is tender.
3 Add the tomatoes, chillies and stock. Season and simmer for 45–60 minutes.
4 Serve hot on *pap* (porridge) or mashed potatoes, with *morogo* (*see* pages 38, 42 and 64) or spinach.

> Morogo is a generic term for wild leaves. Leaves from the bean plant, beetroot leaves or sweet potato leaves can also be used for morogo.

MOROGO WITH TURNIPS AND POTATOES

SERVES 4–6

2 bunches morogo
1 bunch spring onions, chopped
1 bunch turnips, peeled and diced
3 potatoes, peeled and diced
water
salt and pepper to taste
45 g (1½ oz)/45 ml (3 T) butter/margarine

1 Rinse *morogo* thoroughly and chop finely.
2 Place *morogo*, spring onions, turnips, potatoes and a little water in a saucepan. Season with salt and pepper.
3 Let it boil and then simmer gently for about 30 minutes until cooked.
4 Add the butter/margarine and mix well. Serve hot on *pap*.

OPPOSITE *Morogo with Turnips and Potatoes, and Pap*

SWAZILAND
SOUTH AFRICA

Bordered by South Africa in the north, south and west, and by Mozambique in the east, Swaziland is one of the world's smallest countries. It sits on the edge of the southern African escarpment, with the rugged mountains in the west sloping down toward the low-lying plains in the east.

The Swazis, once part of the Dlamini clan who were led across the Lebombo mountains in the mid-eighteenth century by Ngwane I, is one

of three remaining monarchies on the continent. Swaziland's first king, Sobhuza I, gathered refugees fleeing from the Zulu and merged these with his own people, thus building a strong military nation that managed to withstand the onslaught of Shaka. Taking their name from one of the founders of the nation, Mswati I, they waged wars against many neighbouring nations, but eventually succumbed to British rule, finally gaining their independence in 1968. The Swazis speak mainly isiSwati and English and are led today by King Mswati III, who is much revered by his people.

Even in the modern nation, it is quite common to see men and women draped in colourful traditional fabric, called *amahiya*, and the local craftmarkets also abound with the traditional regalia of a people fiercely protective of their cultural heritage.

I visited a rural village and a chief's homestead, where I had the opportunity to experience the humble lifestyle of the people. I watched my hostess grind her maize on the stone and cook an authentic Swazi porridge and Africa's favourite traditional vegetable, *umbidzo* or *igusha*.

Pulses are popular among the Swazi: round beans and lentils are cooked with maize-meal to prepare *lusontfwana* and *tinhlumaya nemphuphu* respectively. Boiled *tindlubu* (round beans) or *umbhonyo* (nuts) are cooled and then shelled and eaten. Maize is enjoyed in many forms: *imbasha* (half-dry roasted maize, mixed with dry nuts, which are then pan-fried), *tinkobe* (dried maize kernels cooked in salted water and allowed to cool before being eaten), and *lukhotse* (fried maize kernels with nuts that are ground and mixed with water). Another favourite is *tincheke*, boiled pumpkin wedges sprinkled with sugar.

LEFT *A Swazi man in tribal dress.*

ABOVE *A woman and child wearing the colourful amahiya, the traditional Swazi cloth.*

OPPOSITE *Villages dotted across the mountain slopes.*

ULUSU NAMAZAMBANE

TRIPE AND POTATO STEW

SERVES 4–6

1 kg (2½ lb) tripe, washed and cut into pieces

water

4 potatoes, quartered

1 onion, chopped

15 ml (1 T) curry powder

5 ml (1 t) salt

1 Cover the tripe with water, bring to the boil
and then simmer for 3 hours.
2 Add potatoes, onion, curry powder and salt.
3 Simmer for a further 30 minutes until the
potatoes are cooked through. Serve with spinach
porridge (*see* this page).

ISIJABANE

SPINACH PORRIDGE

SERVES 4

5 spinach leaves, cut into pieces

1 onion, grated

pinch of salt

1 litre (4 cups) water

240 g (9 oz)/500 ml (2 cups) maize-meal

1 Place the spinach pieces in a saucepan, add
the grated onion and the salt, and cover with
the water.
2 Bring to the boil and then cook for 5 minutes.
3 Add the maize-meal and stir to mix.
4 Let the porridge simmer over a low heat for
about 30 minutes, stirring frequently until
cooked through.
VARIATION: Diced pumpkin can be used instead
of spinach. Serve with milk.

SIDLWADLWA WITH SAMP

MEAT AND VEGETABLE STEW

SERVES 6–8

300 g (11 oz)/375 ml (1½ cups) samp

750 ml (3 cups) water

125 ml (½ cup) oil

1 kg (2½ lb) beef, diced

2 tomatoes, diced

500 ml (2 cups) shredded cabbage

375 ml (1½ cups) crushed peanuts

salt and pepper to taste

1 Soak the samp overnight in cold water.
Drain and cover with fresh water. Cook for
about 1½ hours until soft.
2 In another pot, heat the oil and brown the
beef. Add the tomatoes, cabbage and crushed
peanuts. Season with salt and pepper. Stew for
15 minutes. Mix the stew with the samp. Serve
with spinach porridge (*see* this page).

LEFT *Artistic Swazi wood carving.*

OPPOSITE *Tripe and Potatoes; Isijabane*

SAMP AND BEANS WITH NUTS

SERVES 4

200 g (7 oz)/250 ml (1 cup) samp

200 g (7 oz)/250 ml (1 cup) dry butter beans

water

150 g (5 oz)/250 ml (1 cup) unsalted peanuts

3 chicken stock cubes

salt and pepper to taste

125 ml (½ cup) skim milk powder

75 g (3 oz)/75 ml (5 T) butter/margarine

1 Cover the samp and beans with water and soak overnight. Drain.

2 Place the samp, beans and nuts in a large saucepan and cover with water. Crumble the chicken stock cubes and add to the saucepan. Let it boil and then simmer for 3 hours, adding more water if the samp becomes dry.

3 Season with salt and pepper. Add the milk powder and butter/margarine. Toss together or mash with a wooden spoon.

BEEF STEW

SERVES 4–6

60 ml (4 T) oil

750 g (1½ lb) shin, cut into cubes

45 ml (3 T) flour

salt and pepper to taste

2 onions, chopped

1 garlic clove, crushed

5 ml (1 t) ground cumin

5 ml (1 t) ground coriander

3 potatoes, diced

4 carrots, sliced

1 beef stock cube, dissolved in:

500 ml (2 cups) water

1 Heat the oil, toss the meat in seasoned flour and fry until brown on all sides. Remove the meat and keep warm.

2 Add the onion, garlic, cumin and coriander to the oil and sauté until transparent.

3 Add all the remaining ingredients and heat until boiling. Reduce the heat and simmer for about 45 minutes until cooked through. Serve with samp (*see* this page).

SISHWALA

SUGAR BEAN PORRIDGE

SERVES 4

500 ml (2 cups) sugar beans

water

10 ml (2 t) salt

480 g (17 oz)/1 kg (2½ lb) maize-meal

1 Soak beans overnight in cold water.

2 Drain, cover with fresh water and add salt.
Cook in a large saucepan until soft.

3 Add maize-meal, mix well and cook 30 minutes.

INDLANGALA

CARROT AND GREEN BEAN SOUP

SERVES 4

80 ml (5 T) oil

2 carrots, diced

125 ml (½ cup) green beans

125 ml (½ cup) peanut butter

1 litre (4 cups) water

salt and pepper to taste

1 Heat oil. Add vegetables one at a time and cook
each for 2–3 minutes before adding the next.

2 Add the peanut butter, salt and pepper. Add
water and cook over a low heat for 30 minutes.

NDEBELE
SOUTH AFRICA

The Ndebele, sometimes referred to as the Matabele, are a typical mixture of southern African cultures and this is evident in their blend of staple foods. Descended from the Nguni group – Zulu, Xhosa and Swazi – the Ndebele consist of three groups: one resident in Zimbabwe, and two in the northern provinces of South Africa. The first of the groups migrated from what is today KwaZulu-Natal in about 1600 and, more than two centuries later, another fled north of the Limpopo River. The man responsible for the exodus was Mzilikazi, one of Shaka's Zulu officers, who rebelled against his leader in 1821 and founded the kingdom of the Ndebele. The Ndebele consequently mixed with the Sotho, and today their language has a sprinkling of both Sotho and Afrikaans. The nation is perhaps most noted for its exquisite artwork and striking houses with brilliantly painted walls. Many Ndebele women are gifted artists who have mastered the art of geometric design, most apparent in their traditional costume. They take great pride in their beadwork, and some women wear heavy neckbangles and anklets (iingolwane), and adorn themselves in colourful blankets.

One of my most vivid memories of growing up in the townships is the call of 'Umbila, bakhozi' ('Mealies, my friends') from blanket-clad Ndebele women. They not only sold maize, but also umseme (mats), umthanyelo (short brooms) and colourful hand-woven baskets. I also watched in fascination as my aunt, a traditional Ndebele woman, artistically plastered the floor with cow dung, each time executing a different pattern.

Although the basic Ndebele diet comprises largely maize, beans, umbido, pumpkin and meat, umratha – Ndebele porridge – is a mix of the Venda vhuswa and the Sotho bohobe, while vetkoek – of Dutch/Afrikaans origin, and called amafetkuku by the Ndebele – is enjoyed by many. Uburotho ne konfyt (bread and jam) is a favourite snack. Marula beer is enjoyed during the marula (fruit) season, while other beverages include sorghum beer (ithlodlwa), unotlabalala and marheu. Like other traditional groups who, for centuries, relied on the land for their sustenance, the Ndebele continue to enjoy caterpillars, sand crickets, beetles, flying insects and termites. In summer, before the rain falls, flying ants emerge and are collected, grilled and eaten as a delicacy.

LEFT *The amazingly colourful and intricate Ndebele beadwork.*
ABOVE *A Ndebele woman beading.*
RIGHT *A Ndebele family outside their beautifully painted home.*

1 Clean the offal and cut it into small pieces. Place in a pot and cover with water.

2 Cook the offal over a moderate heat for about 2 hours. Season with salt and pepper.

3 DUMPLINGS: Mix all the ingredients together. Knead for 15 minutes until the dough is elastic. Place the dough in a bowl, cover with plastic and allow to rise in a warm place.

4 Roll the dough into balls the size of golf balls. Place dough balls on meat 30 minutes before the end of the cooking time. Cover the saucepan and simmer until the meat and dumplings are cooked through. Serve hot with vegetables (see, for example the recipe for *umgobhu nombila* below).

ULUSU NAMA DOMBOLO

TRIPE AND SWEETBREADS
WITH DUMPLINGS

SERVES 4

1 kg (2½ lb) sheep offal (tripe, sweetbreads and intestines)

salt and pepper to taste

DUMPLINGS

120 g (4½ oz)/250 ml (1 cup) wholewheat flour

1 packet (10 g) instant dry yeast

salt to taste

15 ml (1 T) lukewarm sugar water

ITHANGA NESIPHILA

PUMPKIN AND MAIZE

SERVES 4

1 small pumpkin, cut into small pieces

fresh maize kernels, cut from 2 cobs

± 125 ml (½ cup) water

5 ml (1 t) sugar (optional)

pinch of salt (optional)

1 Put pumpkin, maize and water in a saucepan.

2 Cook for about 45 minutes, until the maize is tender and the pumpkin is cooked. Stir to mix.

3 Add sugar and salt, if prefered.

IDOMBOLO

WHOLEWHEAT DUMPLINGS

SERVES 4

240 g (9 oz)/500 ml (2 cups) wholewheat flour
(nutty wheat)

1 packet (10 g) instant dry yeast

5 ml (1 t) sugar

pinch of salt

± 250 ml (1 cup) lukewarm water

1 Sift the dry ingredients together in a large mixing bowl.

2 Slowly add the lukewarm water and mix well to form a soft, pliable dough.

3 Knead the dough well for 10 minutes, cover with plastic and allow to rise for 45 minutes until it has doubled in size.

4 Knock the dough down by kneading it, put it in a greased enamel bowl and allow it to rise again until double in size.

5 Place the bowl in a saucepan with boiling water. Cover the saucepan tightly and steam for 1 hour.

Ditloo or jugo beans are round, shiny beans often simply referred to as 'traditional beans'. They have a rich, creamy taste and can be served on their own as a snack, as a side dish or added to soups.

DITLOO/IZINDLUBU

JUGO BEANS

SERVES 4

2 kg (4½ lb) ditloo

500 ml (2 cups) water

salt to taste

1 Cook the ditloo in the water for about 30 minutes, until tender.

2 Season and serve in small bowls, like peanuts.

COW HEEL SOUP

SERVES 4–6

1 kg (2½ lb) cow trotters, cleaned and cut into portions (ask your butcher to clean and slice them)

2 litres (3½ pints/8 cups) water

1 kg (2½ lb) butter beans, soaked overnight

20 ml (4 t) curry powder

salt and pepper to taste

1 Cover the trotters with the water and cook for 1 hour or until half-cooked.

2 Add the butter beans, curry powder, salt and pepper. Simmer for a further hour, until the beans are tender, adding more water if necessary.

3 Serve hot with dumplings (*see ulusu nama dombolo* and *idombolo*, page 52), bread or porridge.

UMQOMBOTHI (ITHLODLWA)

SORGHUM BEER

MAKES 8 LITRES (14 PINTS)

6 kg (13½ lb) sorghum

3 kg (6½ lb) maize-meal

4 litres (7 pints) boiling water

4 litres (7 pints) cold water

1 packet (10 g) brewer's yeast

1 Mix 3 kg (6½ lb) sorghum with the maize-meal and add the boiling water. Leave to cool. Stir in 1 kg (2½ lb) sorghum. Allow the mixture to stand overnight.

2 Place the mixture in a large saucepan, add 1 litre (4 cups) cold water and boil together for 1 hour. Leave to cool.

3 When the mixture is cold, pour it into a large bucket and add the remaining 2 kg (4½ lb) sorghum. Add the rest of the cold water and mix well.

4 Add the brewer's yeast and stir to mix all the ingredients.

5 Cover the mixture with a piece of plastic or a damp cloth and allow to stand for at least 12 hours to brew.

6 Strain the mixture well. Serve cold.

This is a popular African beer, associated with all forms of celebrations and casual drinking. It is highly intoxicating, and is enjoyed by adults only. Children are allowed a tiny sip only if there is an ancestral feast. The beverage that is enjoyed by the whole family is *mageu* (see page 60). Both *umqombothi* and *mageu* are readily available from bottle stores and supermarkets.

SWEET-SOUR BEETROOT SALAD

SERVES 4–6

4 medium beetroot

1 small onion, grated

1 apple, grated

20 ml (4 t) mild chutney

80 g (3 oz)/100 ml (¼–½ cup) sugar

10 ml (2 t) cornflour

75 ml (5 T) vinegar

75 ml (5 T) water

pinch of salt

1 Wash the beetroot well and cook for 30–60 minutes, or until tender.

2 Put the cooked beetroot in cold water for a few minutes before removing the skins.

3 Dice or slice the beetroot and add the onion, apple and chutney.

4 Mix together the sugar, cornflour, vinegar, water and salt. Boil until the sauce thickens.

5 Pour the sauce over the beetroot and allow the salad to cool before serving.

CHAKALAKA SALAD

SERVES 4–6

50 ml (3 T) oil

1 onion, grated

2 garlic cloves, crushed

30 ml (2 T) crushed ginger

1 green pepper, grated

3 green chillies, deseeded and chopped

10 ml (2 t) curry powder

3 medium carrots, grated

1 medium cauliflower, divided into florets

1 tin (410 g/14 oz) baked beans

salt and pepper to taste

1 Heat the oil and sauté the onion, garlic, ginger and green pepper with the chillies and curry powder for 5 minutes.

2 Add the carrots and cauliflower. Cook gently for about 15 minutes or until all the vegetables are cooked.

3 Add the beans and seasoning, heat through and allow to cool. Serve cold.

This salad is similar to atjar, and can be kept in the fridge for several days.

VENDA
SOUTH AFRICA

Steeped in custom and tradition, many of the Venda still believe that the powerful spirits of dead chiefs live in Lake Funduzi in the Soutpansberg and that these spirits can control the crops and the rains. To please their respected ancestors, people must walk back-wards toward the lake and bow low – and no one is allowed to wash or swim in the waters. The tranquil yet spectacular Phiphidi Falls near Thohoyandou are also considered sacred by the Venda people, and their traditional culture still thrives in this valley of legends.

Unlike the other groups of South Africa, the Venda people migrated from the north. History has it that the Karanga-Rozwi people moved south from what is now Zimbabwe and settled

in the northeastern region of South Africa, which was later to become the Venda homeland. These gifted craftsmen smelted iron and created metal implements, which they used to cultivate the land rather than farm with cattle.

Venda, since reincorporated into South Africa, lies in the Limpopo valley and the hub of activity is centred around what was the homeland capital of Thohoyandou ('head of the elephant'). The Limpopo River, which forms the northern border of South Africa, provides much-needed water to the arid lands through which it flows, supporting a series of small, thriving farming villages.

Venda food is simple, yet rich in flavour. *Dofhi* (peanut sauce) forms the basis of many dishes. *Mashonzha* (mopane worms), *tshisevho* (dried meat) and *mukusule* (wild leaves or *morogo*) are cooked in this piquant sauce and served with *vhutete* or *vhuswa* (porridge). Out of courtesy, guests are obliged to use their fingers – as in most of Africa, the hands are washed in warm water and dried before you can partake in the meal.

Making Venda porridge is an art unto itself, and I watch with envy as Masindi stirs and moulds the mixture. In just one week, she built

the rural Venda hut that acts as her kitchen with her own hands. According to custom, all meals are cooked on an open fire on the kitchen floor, which still smells of fresh cow dung. Masindi's grandmother has the daunting task of grinding the nuts and sifting them to ensure a perfect texture. *Vhutete* has to be smooth and completely free of lumps – and, according to the expert, has to be made from 'Special No. 1' maize-meal.

Several herbs and spices are grown in the Venda region and these have been used for many centuries to enhance the flavour and aroma of traditional food. Among these are *lunonya* (caraway seeds) and *mufhoho* (a grain similar to mustard seeds), while *rooibos* tea is also grown in the area. This part of southern Africa is also abundantly blessed with the tropical fruits so often sold at roadside stalls here.

LEFT *An old Venda woman blowing a kudu horn.*
ABOVE *A Venda woman and young maiden.*
OPPOSITE *The spectacular Phiphidi Falls near Thohoyandou.*

DRIED MUKUSULE WITH DOFHI

DRIED MOROGO WITH PEANUT SAUCE

SERVES 4

1 kg (2½ lb) dried leaves

250 ml (1 cup) water

salt and pepper to taste

DOFHI

125 ml (½ cup) ground nuts

250 ml (1 cup) water

1 Rinse the *mukusule* under cold running water
and drain.

2 Place the *mukusule* in a saucepan with the
water and cook until soft.

3 In the meantime, make the *dofhi* by simmering
the ground nuts in the water for 15 minutes
until creamy.

4 Mix the *mukusule* into the ground nut sauce
and simmer gently to combine the flavours. Season with salt and pepper.

TSHISEVHO

DRIED MEAT STEW

SERVES 4

500 g (18 oz) dried meat (biltong)

rough salt to taste

250 ml (1 cup) water

125 ml (½ cup) ground nuts (peanuts crushed in a
traditional pestle and mortar, and sifted)

1 Cook the pieces of dried meat in salted water
until soft. Remove and keep warm.

2 Add the ground nuts to the meat stock, stirring continuously until a smooth sauce is formed.

3 Return the cooked dried meat to the pot and
heat through to blend the flavours.

Traditionally meat dried at home is used for
this dish. If a lot of meat is left over after a
celebration, it is cut into strips and dried in the
sun for a few days. It is then kept and used
when needed. Thick biltong can be used instead
of home-dried meat.

MASHONZHA

MOPANE WORMS WITH TOMATO AND ONION STEW

SERVES 4

250 ml (1 cup) dried mopane worms

500 ml (2 cups) hot water

500 ml (2 cups) boiling water

1 medium onion, chopped

20 ml (4 t) cooking oil

salt and pepper to taste

2 medium tomatoes, diced

pinch of chilli powder

1 Soak the dried mopane worms in hot water for about 3 hours.

2 Remove the mopane worms from the water and place them in a saucepan.

3 Add the boiling water and cook until most of the water has been absorbed.

4 Add oil and onions, season with salt and pepper, and simmer for about 5 minutes.

5 Add the tomatoes and chilli powder, cover and simmer for 10 minutes.

6 Serve hot with fermented porridge (*see* the recipes for fermented *vhuswa*, this page). VARIATION: The onion stew can be replaced with peanut sauce (*dofhi*). (*see* the recipe for *mukusule* on page 58.)

Mopane worms are a delicacy among the Venda, Tsonga and Pedi people. These worms drop from the mopane tree, after which they are named. It is definitely an acquired taste, but once you have learnt to like them you will thoroughly enjoy their nutty taste. *Mashonzha* can be eaten dried or cooked in a stew. Similar to the dried meat and *mukusule*, mopane worms are sun dried and kept for quite a long time.

Super maize-meal is ordinary refined maize-meal, which is sold in most supermarkets. Special maize-meal is commonly referred to as 'No. 1' and is available from selected shops. It is highly refined and looks a lot like flour.

FERMENTED VHUSWA

PORRIDGE

SERVES 4

360 g (12 oz)/750 ml (3 cups) super maize-meal

1 litre (4 cups) lukewarm water

1 litre (4 cups) boiling water

1 kg (2½ lb) special maize-meal

1 Soak the super maize-meal in lukewarm water, cover and leave to ferment for 2 days.

2 Pour boiling water into a saucepan and add 500 ml (2 cups) of the fermented water.

3 Bring the water to the boil and add the fermented maize-meal paste. Simmer gently, stirring until the mixture thickens.

4 Cover the saucepan and cook the mixture over a low heat for 10 minutes. Add small quantities of the special maize-meal, mixing thoroughly to avoid lumps.

5 Cover and simmer for a further 15 minutes, stirring the porridge constantly.

VHUTETWE/VHUSWA

1 litre (4 cups) water

240 g (9 oz)/500 ml (2 cups) maize-meal

1 Bring the water to the boil and slowly add the maize-meal. Stir thoroughly with a whisk until smooth.

2 Pound the mixture with a wooden spoon to ensure that no lumps remain. Cook for about 20 minutes, pounding and stirring, until the porridge is cooked through.

3 Pour layers of hot porridge on a plate to resemble stacked thick pancakes. Leave the porridge to cool and eat it with your hand.

> Usually 'Special No. 1' maize-meal is used for this porridge. The porridge is cooked in the morning and kept all day. The layers come off easily and the porridge is kept covered so that it stays moist. It is eaten with *mukusule* (morogo) and *mashonza* (mopane worms) and meat stews.

SPINACH AND MUKUSULE MIX

SERVES 4

1 bunch spinach leaves

1 bunch beetroot leaves

1 bunch pumpkin leaves

1 large potato, quartered

60 ml (4 T) butter/margarine

salt and masala to taste

1 Wash the leaves thoroughly, rinse, chop and place in a saucepan.

2 Add the potato, onion, water, salt and masala. Cook for 20 minutes or until the potato is soft.

3 Add butter/margarine. Mash until well mixed.

MAGEU

MAKES 1 LITRE (1½ PINTS)

750 ml (3 cups) water

120 g (4½ oz)/250 ml (1 cup) maize-meal

60 ml (4 T) flour

sugar to taste

1 Boil the water in a saucepan.

2 Mix a little cold water with the maize-meal to make a paste.

3 Add the paste to the boiling water and stir to mix. Turn down the heat and simmer gently, stirring constantly until cooked. Leave to cool.

4 Add the flour and sugar, mix well and leave to stand for two days.

5 Taste to see whether the mixture is sour. If not, leave it to stand for another day. Dilute with water, if necessary, and then serve.

CHICKEN-FEET STEW

Serves 4–6

6 chicken feet, cleaned

6 chicken heads, cleaned

500 g (18 oz) chicken intestine, cleaned

45 ml (3 T) oil

1 large tomato, grated

1 green pepper, chopped

water

salt and masala to taste

1 Cover the meat with water and heat until boiling. Lower the heat and simmer gently for about 30 minutes until cooked,.

2 Heat the oil and fry the green pepper until soft. Add the tomato, salt and masala.

3 Add tomato gravy to the meat and simmer for 15 minutes.

4 Serve with potato *pap* (porridge) or dumplings (*see* recipes for *ulusu nama dombolo* and *idombolo* on page 52).

BOTSWANA

Landlocked Botswana, surrounded by Zimbabwe, South Africa and Namibia, is a thriving country, rich in diamonds, wildlife and talented, friendly people. The small eastern section that includes part of the Limpopo River is home to 80 per cent of the Batswana.

The land here is extremely fertile, whereas the huge western area is mostly too dry for dependable agriculture and cannot, therefore, sustain any more than a sparse population. Rainfall throughout the country is both sparse and erratic, and Botswana is frequently plagued by drought.

The first Tswana speakers, the Kwena, entered what is now Botswana from the south in the 18th century, but the Ngwaketse and the Ngwato soon broke away. The Tswana, in turn, then broke from the Ngwato, and by the nineteenth century the Tswana were well established in the area. Botswana finally gained its independence from Britain in 1966, and it has remained a largely tranquil country, where the government functions on democratic principles. This relative calm has since given rise to exciting developments in the tourist industry, which is built around the country's abundant wildlife resources, most notably in the northern regions.

Most Batswana generally hold other people in high regard and believe a man's worth is measured by the way he treats others (*motho ke motho ka batho*). Unannounced visitors are seldom considered intruders, and are always given something to eat: *Moeng goroga re je ka wena* (When guests arrive, we eat).

My hostess in Botswana was MaDinko, a traditional Motswana woman, who taught me how to cook the real Setswana *mosoko*, or porridge commonly known as *bogobe bating* and *morogo*.

The Setswana diet consists mainly of *bogobe*, *legola* (grain sorghum), and *sebube* (grain sorghum porridge cooked in sour milk). *Ting* (fermented porridge) made from plain maize meal or *mabele* meal is also a firm favourite, while chopped *diretlo /serobe* (tripe), *seswaa* (pounded meat) and *phane* (mopane worms) are popular accompaniments to the meal. As with most African groups, *morogo* is eaten in abundance, the most popular version being made from leaves of the bean plant. *Dinawa* (dried beans), *ditloo* (jugo beans) and *letlhodi* (lentils) are boiled in salted water and seasoned with salt and pepper also form part of the daily Setswana menu.

LEFT *Baines' Baobabs at the northern tip of the Kudaikm Pan.*
ABOVE *A man poling a mokoro, typical of the region.*
OPPOSITE *A large herd of buffalo on the Okavango Delta.*

SESWAA

POUNDED MEAT

SERVES 6

1 kg (2½ lb) brisket

water

1 large onion, chopped

salt and pepper to taste

1 Place the brisket, the onion and seasoning in a saucepan. Cover with water and cook about 2½ hours until soft.

2 Drain liquid and pound the meat until flaky. Remove the bones. Serve with porridge, *morogo* (*see* this page and pages 38 and 42) and gravy

MOROGO

SERVES 4

1 kg (2½ lb) bean leaves

2 onions, chopped

125 ml (½ cup) water

15 ml (1 T) oil

salt and pepper to taste

1 Place the *morogo* and chopped onion in a saucepan and add the water and oil.

2 Boil for 15 minutes, stirring continuously. Season with salt and pepper.

For *morogo*, use plant leaves, preferably bean plants. The leaves are blanched and then sun dried. Shops in Botswana sell dried bean leaves.

VENISON RAGOUT

SERVES 4–6

1 leg of impala of 750 g–1 kg (1½–2½ lb),
deboned and cut into cubes

2 onions, chopped

2 ripe tomatoes, grated

62,5 ml (½ cup) oil

250 ml (1 cup) beef stock

salt and pepper to taste

250 g (½ lb) button mushrooms

1 litre (4 cups) cream

50 ml (4 T) red wine

30 ml (2 T) cranberry sauce, optional

1 Combine the cubed impala, onions, tomatoes, oil and stock. Simmer for 1 hour until soft.
2 Remove the meat from the stock and place in another saucepan. (Keep stock to make soup.) Season. Add the mushrooms, red wine and cream.
3 Cook slowly until creamy and thickened. Spoon into a serving dish, garnish with chopped parsley and cranberry sauce.
4 Serve with rice and vegetables in season.

1 Sift together the flour, baking powder and salt. Add the sugar and rub the butter/margarine into the mixture until it resembles breadcrumbs.
2 Beat the egg and milk together, gradually add the mixture to the flour and mix to make a pliable soft dough.
3 Roll the dough out lightly until it is about 10 mm (½ in) thick. Cut into scone shapes with a dough cutter.
4 Place on a greased baking sheet. Bake at 220 °C (425 °F/gas 7) for 12–15 minutes.

> These scones differ from the cream and jam type
> – they are heavier due to the method of mixing.
> They are usually enjoyed with ginger beer

GINGER BEER

MAKES 5 LITRES (8½ PINTS)
5 litres (8½ pints) boiling water
240 g (8 oz)/300 ml (1½ cup) sugar
30 ml (2 T) ground ginger
10 ml (2 t) active dry yeast
15 ml (1 T) tartaric acid
15 ml (1 T) cream of tartar
250 ml (1 cup) raisins

TRADITIONAL SCONES

MAKES 12
240 g (9 oz)/500 ml (2 cups) cake flour
20 ml (4 t) baking powder
pinch of salt
80 ml (6 T) sugar
125 g (4½ oz)/125 ml (½ cup) butter/margarine
1 egg
150 ml (½ cup) milk

1 Pour boiling water into a large saucepan. Add sugar, stir to dissolve and add the ginger. Simmer for about 30 minutes. Leave until lukewarm.
2 Add all the remaining ingredients. Cover and keep in a warm place for 2 days to mature.
3 Chill before serving.

BOHOBE BATING YAMABELE

SOUR PORRIDGE

SERVES 4
2,5 litres (4 1/3 pints/10 cups) water
4 x 250 ml (4 cups) fermented ting paste

1 Heat the water to boiling point, pour half the *ting* paste into the boiling water and stir constantly to avoid lumps.
2 When the paste is smooth, let it cook slowly for about 10 minutes, stirring occasionally.
3 Add the rest of the paste. Cook for a further 30 minutes, stirring constantly. Serve with *morogo* (*see* pages 38, 42 and 64) or meat.

> *Mosoko, ting* or sour porridge is a typical Batswana
> meal. To prepare *ting* paste, take any quantity of
> super maize meal or *mabele a ting* and mix with
> warm water. Cover and leave to ferment overnight.

OSTRICH KEBABS

SERVES 4–6

500 g (18 oz) ostrich fillet, cubed

2 onions, chopped

3 green peppers, diced

salt and pepper to taste

250 ml (1 cup) bought pepper sauce

cranberry sauce (optional)

1 Thread the ostrich fillet, onions and peppers
on skewers. Season with salt and pepper.

2 Grill the kebabs over medium heat for about
10 minutes.

3 Mix the pepper sauce with cranberry sauce,
if prefered, and serve over the kebabs. Serve the
kebabs with rice and vegetables in season

ZIMBABWE

This landlocked country lies entirely within the tropics and has been blessed with a balmy climate. Rainfall blows in from the east, drenching the spectacular highlands, but diminishes as the moist air moves west. But Zimbabwe has been equally blessed with a rich and proud cultural history. There are many Stone Age rock paintings, and archaeologists can trace humankind's occupation of what is now Zimbabwe to 100 000 years ago. By the twelfth century, the Shona people were building with stone, initiating a unique African tradition that left Great Zimbabwe and other megalithic sites scattered around the country.

The Shona constitute some 75 per cent of the total population of around 8 million. The second largest group are the Nguni-speaking Ndebele, who, led by Mzilikazi, made their grand entrance into Zimbabwe around the nineteenth century and established themselves around Bulawayo.

Boasting the world-famous Victoria Falls, the great Zambezi River, Kariba and some of Africa's finest game parks, the people of Zimbabwe are also some of the continent's most creative, and most of the rural folk are expert crafters. On my visit to Zimbabwe, I spent some time with one such family. Sonile Ncube, a single mother of seven, supports her family by selling the *hoso* (musical instruments) she finely crafts from a fruit known as *umkhemeswane*. Her elder son carves hippos and other animals from wood, the younger siblings smooth and polish them, and they are then sold along the road or to craft markets in town.

Sonile's kitchen is an extension of her artistic abilities. Neatly carved shelves adorn the walls of her mud hut. Large canisters of grains line up on the clean floor, on which neat patterns were drawn with cow dung. Pots and pans take their pride of place on the mud shelves. The staple diet of most Zimbabweans is *sadza* (porridge) made from maize-meal, with *rape* (a type of wild leaf) and *okra* common side dishes, while nuts – ground and whole – form a major part of the menu.

Kapenta, a tiny fish found mainly in the Zambezi, is eaten throughout the country, as is *amacimbi* (mopane worms). Both are sun dried and stored until needed, and are prepared in much the same way: sautéed in oil and served on *sadza* or added to a tomato-and-onion stew.

LEFT *Tribal dancers at Victoria Falls.*

ABOVE *Zimbabwe is famous for its stone and wooden carvings.*

OPPOSITE *Aerial view of the Zambezi Gorge at Victoria*

NYAMA

TRADITIONAL BEEF STEW

SERVES 4

1 kg (2½ lb) brisket or chuck, cut into portions

salt to taste

500 ml (2 cups) water

2 onions, chopped

2 tomatoes, chopped

salt and pepper to taste

4 x 250 ml (4 cups) rape or *chimolia*

(*morogo*), shredded

1 Boil the meat in salted water until it is cooked
and soft.

2 Add the onion and tomato, salt and pepper,
and *rape* or *chimolia* (*morogo*).

3 Simmer gently for about 20 minutes until
the vegetables are cooked through. Serve with
sadza, the Zimbabwean version of porridge
(*see* the recipe for *nshima* on page 84 for the
Zambian version).

PUMPKIN IN PEANUT SAUCE

SERVES 4

125 ml (½ cup) water

½ pumpkin, peeled and cut into small portions

60 ml (4 T) peanut butter

1 Heat the water in a saucepan to boiling
point and add the pumpkin. Cook until soft,
stirring occasionally.

2 Add the peanut butter and stir to mix.
Mash until smooth.

CHUMUKUYU

DRIED MEAT

1 kg (2½ lb) lean sirloin of beef

10 ml (2 t) salt

5 ml (1 t) black pepper

5 ml (1 t) cayenne pepper

3 ml (½ t) peri peri

60 ml (4 T) olive oil

1 Preheat the oven to 140° C (275° F/gas 1).

2 Remove the gristle and sinew from the meat.
Cut the meat into strips.

3 Lay the meat on a baking tray and season
it with salt, black pepper, cayenne pepper and
peri peri. Drizzle the olive oil over the meat.

4 Place the baking tray in the preheated oven,
and leave the meat to dry for 30 minutes. Leave
outside for at least 12 hours to dry completely.
Serve as a snack.

CHUMUKUYU STEW

DRIED MEAT STEW

SERVES 4

12 pieces of dried meat, 300–500 g (11–18 oz)

water

60 g (2½ oz)/60 ml (4 T) butter/margarine

1 onion, sliced

1 garlic clove, crushed

4 ripe tomatoes, chopped

salt and pepper to taste

75 ml (5 T) peanut butter

1 packet of beef soup powder

250 ml (1 cup) water

1 Cover the dried meat with water and cook
until tender.

2 Melt the butter/margarine and sauté the
onion and garlic until transparent. Add the
tomatoes. Season with salt and pepper.

3 Mix together the peanut butter, soup powder
and water. Add the mixture to the stew and
simmer gently for 5 minutes.

4 Add the cooked beef to the stew and mix
well. Cook for 10 minutes until the flavours are
blended. Serve on *sadza* (the Zimbabwean stiff
porridge; *see* the recipe for *nshima* on page 84 for
the Zambian version) or dumplings (*see* page 52)
with fried brown mushrooms.

CREAMY SWEET POTATOES

SERVES 4–6

4 sweet potatoes
125 ml (½ cup) whipped cream
1 tin (397 g/14 oz) condensed milk
62,5 ml (¼ cup) raisins

1 Rinse the sweet potatoes under running water. Place them in a saucepan, cover with water and boil in their jackets until cooked through.
2 Peel the cooked sweet potatoes and mash until smooth.
3 Stir in the whipped cream, condensed milk and raisins. Serve with more whipped cream or custard for an unusual, delicious desert.

OKRA IN PEANUT SAUCE

SERVES 4

125 ml (½ cup) water
250 g (9 oz) fresh okra, sliced
2 ml (½ t) bicarbonate of soda
1 large tomato, grated
salt and pepper to taste
75 ml (5 T) finely pounded roasted peanuts

1 Heat the water to boiling point, add the okra and bicarbonate of soda. Cook for 10 minutes. Add the tomato, salt and pepper.
2 Mix the ground nuts with a little water, add it to the okra and cook for a further 15 minutes. Serve with porridge (*see* the recipe for *vhuswa* on page 60).

Okra is a popular vegetable in most parts of Africa. The small variety is nicer for cooking. This vegetable is very nutritious and is best eaten with *sadza* (porridge) .

MAWUYU, UMKHOMO

BAOBAB FRUIT IN CREAM

8 baobab fruits
125 ml (½ cup) milk
100 g (4 oz)/125 ml (½ cup) sugar
250 ml (1 cup) whipped cream

1 Break the baobab fruits in half. Remove the floury seeds and place them in a bowl.
2 Add the milk, sugar and whipped cream to form a thick consistency. Serve as dessert.
VARIATION: Condensed milk can be used instead of milk and sugar.

CHICKEN IN PEANUT SAUCE

Serves 4–6

1 whole chicken of 750g–1 kg (1½–2½ lb)

45 ml (3 T) seasoned flour

60 ml (4 T) oil

1 large onion, chopped

1 garlic clove, crushed

15 ml (1 T) crushed ginger

1 green pepper, chopped

2 large tomatoes, peeled and diced

1 chicken stock cube, dissolved in:

250 ml (1 cup) water

salt and pepper to taste

5 ml (1 t) rosemary

200 g (7 oz)/125 ml (½ cup) peanut butter

1 Cut the chicken into portions and toss in the seasoned flour.

2 Heat the oil and brown the chicken. Remove the chicken from the saucepan and keep warm.

3 Sauté onion, garlic and ginger until transparent.

4 Add green pepper and tomatoes. Return chicken to saucepan. Add stock, seasoning and rosemary. Bring to the boil and then simmer for 30 minutes.

5 Add the peanut butter and continue to cook over a low heat for a further 15 minutes. Add a little water if the stew is too thick. Serve with porridge (*see* the recipe for *vhuswa* on page 60).

MOZAMBIQUE

Mozambique's long and languid shoreline stretches over 2 000 kilometres along the Indian Ocean, while the interior extends along the Zambezi valley to Zimbabwe and Zambia, with the southern tip of Malawi driving a wedge into Mozambican territory. Two of Africa's major rivers – the Limpopo and Zambezi – also flow through Mozambique.

During the country's wet season, it is both hot and humid, with temperatures rising up to 29 °C on the coast. The dry season runs from April to September, and it is during these months that the temperature is the most pleasant.

Although the Portuguese first arrived here as long ago as the fifteenth century, their early activities were restricted to setting up trading enclaves and forts along the coast, and the interior remained largely unblemished by colonial influence.

The indigenous communities mostly occupied the inland regions and conducted vigorous trading systems of their own. It was thus only in the seventeenth century that colonisation began to infiltrate, with private owners settling on land granted by the crown of Portugal or taken by the conquest of African chiefs.

Mozambique finally gained its independence from Portugal in 1975, but after so many years of colonial rule, the Portuguese and indigenous cultures have become intertwined and the country's official language remains Portuguese. Most Mozambican cafés and restaurants serve Portuguese food, and the Portuguese influence is also evident in the food eaten by the local people.

Our Mozambican hostess, Joseffina, however, prides herself on her traditional cooking. Everything is done by hand – with the aid of a pestle and mortar, or a coconut squeezer. Joseffina pounds her own cassava flour and grates her own coconut to extract the coconut milk. True to tradition, her young daughter also helps her prepare the food in the family's courtyard kitchen.

As in most African communities, porridge – called *nsima* in Mozambique – is the staple dish, closely followed by the ever-popular rice, most often combined with prawns and called *chiru* (pilau).

Chiguinha is a mixture of cassava flour and ground peanuts, which are mixed together and simmered over a gentle heat.

LEFT *Mozambique is famous for its fish and seafood.*
ABOVE *A young Mozambican girl.*
OPPOSITE *A typical coastal scene near Vilancolus.*

BIFE A CARDOSO

BEEF CARDOSO STYLE

SERVES 1

250 ml (1 cup) water

300 g (11 oz) rump steak

salt and pepper to taste

1 medium onion

1 medium carrot

1 bay leaf

250 g (9 oz) white cabbage, sliced

20 ml (4 t) olive oil

300 g (11 oz) potatoes

2 eggs, fried

black olives to garnish

1 Boil 125 ml (½ cup) of the water. Add the meat, onion, carrot and bay leaf. Season and cook for 20 minutes.

2 Boil cabbage with 10 ml (2 t) of the olive oil.

3 Boil the potatoes in 125 ml water.

4 Slice the beef into three equal pieces, arrange on the bed of cabbage, alternating with the two fried eggs, and drizzle rest of olive oil over.

6 Serve with boiled potatoes, and the carrot and onion from the stock. Garnish with black olives.

A typical Mozambican dish, in which the Portuguese influence is evident.

GALINHA A PIRI PIRI

PERI PERI CHICKEN

SERVES 2

1 chicken of approximately 1,3 kg (2½ lb)

salt and pepper

200 g (7 oz)/200 ml (½ cup) butter

6 whole fresh peri peri or hot chillies, crushed

20 ml (4 t) lemon juice

4 cloves garlic, crushed

5 ml (1 t) paprika

20 ml (4 t) olive oil

SAUCE

20 g (1 oz)/20 ml (4 t) butter

10 ml (2 t) olive oil

2 cloves garlic

ground peri peri to taste

juice of 1 lemon

15 ml (1 T) chopped parsley

1 Clean chicken, cut through back and flatten. Remove the carcass. Slit through the thick parts.
2 Mix the rest of ingredients to a paste. Rub it over the inside and outside of the chicken.
3 Marinate the chicken for 2 hours, then grill or braai, basting and turning it frequently.
4 SAUCE: Fry garlic in butter and olive oil. Add rest of ingredients. Remove garlic, pour sauce over chicken and serve with rice and vegetables.

CAMARÃO GRELHADO MATAPA

MOROGO WITH PRAWNS

SERVES 4

1 kg (2½ lb) *matapa*, rinsed and chopped

100 g (4 oz) peanuts, crushed

250 ml (1 cup) coconut milk

4 tomatoes, peeled and chopped

1 onion, chopped

250 g (9 oz) dried prawns or shrimps

1 Mix all the ingredients in a saucepan.

2 Stew together until the matapa has cooked through. Serve over *nsima*, the Mozambican porridge (*see* the recipe for *nshima* on page 84 for the Zambian version).

> Coconut milk is made by breaking open a whole fresh coconut and shredding the coconut flesh. Mix it with cold water and leave for a few minutes, then squeeze it through a strainer. Alternatively, place desiccated coconut in water and simmer gently. Rub the mixture through a sieve and use the fluid as coconut milk.

> Cassava, a tubular vegetable that looks like a sweet potato, is used in many East and West African dishes. The peel is slit down to the flesh with a sharp knife, and it can be pulled away with the fingers, like a ripe banana peel. The tuber is then washed, rinsed and sliced lengthways to remove the core, which resembles thick string. Plain boiled cassava may replace potatoes in any meal. A variety of savoury and sweet dishes are made from whole cassava or cassava flour.

MUTHUMBULA/ MANDIOCA

CASSAVA

SERVES 4

250 g (9 oz) cassava

2 eggs, beaten

salt and pepper to taste

oil for frying

1 Peel and cut the cassava into serving portions. Boil until soft and cooked through.

2 Dip the cassava in beaten egg and deep-fry in hot oil. Serve as a side dish.

CAMARÃO GRELHADO

GRILLED PRAWNS WITH GARLIC SAUCE

SERVES 1

12 medium-sized prawns

15 ml (1 T) lemon juice

10 ml (2 t) salt

5 whole peri peri or hot chillies, crushed

4 garlic cloves, crushed

20 ml (4 t) olive oil

GARLIC SAUCE

125 g (4½ oz)/125 ml (½ cup) butter

2 cloves garlic, crushed

2 whole peri peri or hot chillies

1 bay leaf

25 ml (2 T) lemon juice

1 Slit the back of each prawn and devein.

2 Mix the lemon juice, salt, peri peri, garlic and olive oil to a paste, press the paste into the cut of the prawn and close. Sprinkle any remaining paste over the prawns and marinate for 3 hours.

3 Grill the prawns for 20 minutes, using the marinade for basting.

4 Melt the butter in a pan, add the garlic, peri peri and bay leaf, and heat until boiling.

5 Remove from heat, add lemon juice and mix well. Serve the prawns and garlic sauce with rice.

SAFFRON RICE SALAD TOPPED WITH MIXED SEAFOOD

ABOVE *Beautifully finished Mozambican wood carving*

SEAFOOD

Mozambique has an extremely long coastline with a warm coastal current which creates an ideal breeding ground for a variety of shellfish. Not surprisingly, prawns feature prominently on their menu and 'LM' prawns are a delicacy famous for both their size and flavour.

SERVES 8

SAFFRON RICE

4 threads saffron

½ onion, chopped

250 ml (1 cup) lukewarm water

15 ml (1T) butter/margarine

150g (5oz)/187,5 ml (¾ cup) basmati rice

62,5 ml (¼ cup) wild rice

250 ml (1 cup) salted water

TOPPING

45 ml (3T) olive or sunflower oil

500g (18oz) selection of seafood

1 clove garlic, crushed

80 ml (5T) white wine

salt and pepper to taste

15 ml (1T) chopped capers

chopped dill

DRESSING

60ml (4T) balsamic vinegar

15 ml (1T) water

salt and pepper to taste

90 ml (6T) olive oil

GARNISH

100g (4 oz) cherry tomatoes

½ cucumber, sliced

1 Mix saffron with 250 ml (1 cup) lukewarm water and set aside.

2 Melt the butter/margarine and lightly sauté the onion. Add the basmati rice and fry together for a few seconds.

3 Add the saffron water and salt and heat until boiling, stirring constantly.

4 Cover until the rice is cooked. Remove from the heat and let it cool.

5 Meanwhile boil the wild rice in the salted water for approximately 20 minutes. Rinse with cold water and drain.

6 TOPPING: Heat the oil in a casserole. Add the seafood mix and crushed garlic, stir to cover and then roast the mixture under strong heat for 1 minute. Add the wine and seasoning. Cover the casserole and cook for 3 minutes. Remove the seafood mix and allow to cool.

7 DRESSING: Mix vinegar and 15 ml (1T) water, season with salt and pepper and whisk in the oil.

8 Mix the saffron rice and wild rice together. Top with the seafood mix, capers and dill.

9 Refrigerate for 1 hour. Leave on the chilled platter, and before serving pour the dressing over and garnish with cherry tomatoes and cucumber slices.

ZAMBIA

Landlocked in the tropics of southern Africa, far from the shores of either the Atlantic or the Indian oceans, lies the Republic of Zambia. Situated on a plateau between 900 and 1 500 metres high, Zambia is studded with lakes and covered with deciduous forest, savanna and marshland, while its rivers and lakes provide abundant fish harvests. The country is primarily open woodland, and rainfall occurs from late November to April. Zambia is blessed with exceptional beauty, and few other countries can boast such natural diversity. The

Victoria Falls, the abundance of mountains, lakes, rivers, forests and wildlife typify Africa and make it extremely alluring to the visitor.

Signs of human habitation here go back some 200 000 years, with the earliest tribes gathering fruits, hunting and fishing to sustain themselves. They were, however, taken under British rule by Cecil John Rhodes, and remained so until the country gained its independence in 1964 by joining the British Commonwealth.

The Zambian population currently stands at nearly 10 million, with the capital, Lusaka, home to about 10% of the people. Although the country's official language remains English, there are a number of indigenous languages, including Bemba (the largest of the groups), Lozi, Nyanja and Tonga. However, despite over 70 different ethnic groups, Zambia is perhaps less affected by ethnic tensions than any African state.

Zambia is one of Africa's most urbanized countries, but while Lusaka is characterised by buzzing markets, the rural population live largely by subsistence farming. The country has an exotic cuisine, with extraordinary flavours and aromas. Its markets – the nerve centre where virtually

the entire community shops – are brimming with all sorts of unusual vegetables. It is here that you will inevitably find fresh produce, live chickens, fresh fish, cooked food, crafts, jewellery and one of Zambia's most renowned exports, the colourful fabric known as *xhitenge*.

During my visit to the country, I spent some time chatting to a local housewife about culture and traditional eating patterns. She showed me how to cook *nshima* (porridge), chicken stew, *lumanda* (okra in peanut sauce), and introduced me to the flavours of Zambian beverages, such as *muukhoyo*, *tombwa* and *kachasu*.

LEFT *A busy produce market near Lusaka.*

ABOVE *An industrious potter hard at work.*

OPPOSITE *The bushveld – showing typical savanna vegetation.*

VENISON SHIN

Serves 6–8

45 ml (3 T) oil

2 kg (4½ lb) shin, cut into thin slices

3 onions, chopped

4 tomatoes, chopped

500 ml (2 cups) water

salt and pepper to taste

1 Heat the oil and brown the meat.

2 Add the onions and tomato, sauté for a few minutes. Add the water. Allow to simmer for 1½ hours, stirring occasionally.

3 Season with salt and pepper, and reduce the sauce by boiling uncovered. Serve on rice or stiff porridge (*see* the recipe for *nshima*, this page).

NSHIMA

STIFF PORRIDGE

Serves 6–8

5 litres (8½ pints) water

salt to taste (optional)

240 g (9 oz)/500 ml (2 cups) maize-meal

1 Heat the water to boiling point. Add salt, if prefered. Gradually add the maize-meal, stirring all the time until it is mixed with the water.

2 Cover and allow to cook over medium heat until cooked through, stirring constantly to avoid burning.

> Porridge is a staple food in most of Africa. It may be prepared in many different ways, which result in a variety of textures, but the basic ingredients remain the same. The amount of water used determines the consistency. For soft porridge, which is served at breakfast, use twice the amount of water as that required for stiff porridge. This stiff porridge, known as *nshima* in Zambia and Malawi, is served at lunch and dinner.

NKUKU

CHICKEN

Serves 8–10

3 kg (6½ lb) chicken

salt and pepper to taste

200 ml (½ cup) oil

1 large onion, chopped

2 large tomatoes, chopped

1 Cut the chicken into portions. Season with salt and pepper.

2 Heat the oil and cook the chicken until brown. Add the onion and brown.

3 Stir in the tomatoes, turn down the heat and stew for 45 minutes. Serve with porridge (*see* the recipe for *nshima*, this page) and sweet potato leaves (*see* the recipe for *kalembula*, page 86).

ANGWALA

WHOLE BREAM

SERVES 8

60 g (2½ oz)/125 ml (½ cup) flour

salt and pepper to taste

4 whole breams

60 ml (4 T) lemon juice

125 ml (½ cup) oil

2 onions, sliced

4 tomatoes, peeled and chopped

2 fresh chillies

1 Mix together the flour, salt and pepper. Brush the fish with the lemon juice and coat with the seasoned flour.

2 Heat the oil in a pan. Pan-fry the fish on both sides for about 10 minutes, or until it is brown and crisp.

3 Place the fried fish on a serving dish and keep it warm.

4 In another pan, mix together the onion, tomatoes and chillies and fry until soft.

5 Serve the fish with the tomato sauce and rice.

> Use any firm white fish, such as hake, as a substitute for *angwala*.

IMPHWA

BABY BRINJAL

SERVES 8

500 ml (2 cups) water

3 onions, chopped

3 tomatoes, chopped

750 ml (3 cups) diced brinjal

salt and pepper to taste

3 ml (½ t) chilli powder

3 ml (½ t) turmeric

1 Boil water in a saucepan, add the onions and tomatoes, and simmer for 10 minutes.

2 Add rest of ingredients. Cook for 20 minutes. Serve with porridge (*see nshima*, page 84).

This dish is mostly eaten in the northern and eastern parts of Zambia.

This is a favourite of the Nsenga people, one of the Zambian tribes

KALEMBULA

SWEET POTATO LEAVES

SERVES 4

500 ml (2 cups) water

3 ripe tomatoes, peeled and chopped

750 ml (3 cups) sweet potato leaves

salt and pepper to taste

1 Boil water, add tomatoes and cook until soft.

2 Add sweet potato leaves and cook 10 minutes more. Season with salt and pepper. Serve with porridge (*see* recipe for *nshima*, page 84).

VARIATION: Make a sauce using freshly ground peanuts and boiling water, add it to the leaves and simmer for 20 minutes. This dish is called *mbyori*.

FUTARI

BAKED SWEET POTATOES

SERVES 8

6 x 250 ml (6 cups) water

2 kg (4½ lb) sweet potatoes, peeled and thinly sliced

salt to taste

PEANUT SAUCE

4 x 250 ml (4 cups) ground nuts

250 ml (1 cup) hot water

1 Boil water in a saucepan. Add sweet potatoes and cook until soft. Drain. Arrange the slices in a baking dish. Season with salt and keep warm.

2 PEANUT SAUCE: Combine the ground nuts and hot water in a small bowl.

4 Pour the sauce on the sweet potatoes and bake at 180 °C (350 °F/gas 4) for 15 minutes.

DELELE

OKRA

SERVES 6

500 ml (2 cups) water
5 ml (1 t) bicarbonate of soda
750 ml (3 cups) okra, sliced
3 tomatoes, peeled and chopped
salt and pepper to taste

1 Bring water to the boil, then add bicarbonate of soda. When dissolved, add the okra.
2 Add the tomatoes and seasoning. Allow to simmer for 15 minutes, stirring occasionally.
3 When the okra boils over, it means it is cooked and ready for serving. Serve with porridge (*see* the recipe for *nshima,* page 84).
VARIATION: Okra can also be cooked in ground nut sauce – freshly ground peanuts mixed with boiling water – to make *lumanda.*

MALAWI

Malawi lives up to its reputation as 'the warm heart of Africa'. Malawians are inevitably kind, gentle and hospitable by nature, and go out of their way to expose their beautiful country to visitors.

Situated along the southern continuation of the great Rift Valley, Malawi consists of a narrow sliver that is densely populated. Its small size and irregular borders are remnants of late nineteenth-century politics that played havoc with the internal affairs of the continent.

Although much of the land is covered with forest and savanna, fishing remains the main industry and major source of income for the people who live along the shore of Lake Malawi, Lake Chilwa and the Shire River. A plantation economy is, however, also vital, and produces tobacco, cotton, tea and groundnuts for export.

The population is over 11 million, but nearly a quarter of a million adult males labour on the Zimbabwean and South African mines or on Zimbabwe's tobacco farms. Malawi became a British Protectorate in 1891 – and independent in 1964 – and English thus remains one of the official languages, along with Chewa.

The markets sell virtually everything – from exotic maroon beads and traditional crafts to mahogany and ebony furniture and of course, thanks to Lake Malawi, plenty of fish. With its inviting blue waters and empty beaches, Lake Malawi is the country's top tourist attraction.

Local cuisine echoes much of what is found elsewhere in southern Africa: *nsima* (porridge), *rape* (the Malawian version of *morogo*), pumpkin leaves, sweet potatoes, the generous use of *nsijiro* (ground nut flour). Another favourite is *chinangwa*, a very filling, potato-like vegetable that is peeled, boiled in salt water, sliced and served with tea instead of bread. Other favourites include okra, Chinese cabbage, *tarpis*, red-skinned potatoes and red onions, all of which grow abundantly here. Because it is the location of the largest lake in Africa, fish features prominently on the local menu, and Malawians eat twice as much fish as meat. The most common fish varieties at the markets are *chambo* (the collective name of six species of tilapia), *kampango* (a larger, tasty fish) and *usipa* (a very small fish, often dried).

Chambo, a favourite that features prominently on hotel and restaurant menus, is prepared in many ways: curried, stewed, grilled whole, or dried. These fish are rather bony, but very tasty.

LEFT *Fishermen at Lake Malawi.*
ABOVE *A woman preparing nshima over an open fire.*
OPPOSITE *Scenic Lake Malawi in the early morning light.*

ABOVE *A chef with a fresh catch of chambo (tilapia)*

Okra (ladies' fingers) are readily available and very cheap in Malawi, especially during the rainy season. They are best used young as they become fibrous and slimy when older. Okra can be cooked with lemon juice to eradicate any sliminess. When buying okra, the ends should snap off crisply, which indicates that they are tender.

MBATATA

SWEET POTATO AND MINCE BAKE

60 ml (4 T) oil
2 large sweet potatoes, peeled and thinly sliced
1 bunch spring onions, chopped
500 g (18 oz) minced beef
4 tomatoes, peeled and chopped
1 tin (75 g/3 oz) tomato paste
15 ml (1 T) vinegar
salt and pepper to taste
breadcrumbs

CHEESE SAUCE
30 ml (2 T) butter/margarine
15 ml (1 T) flour
250 ml (1 cup) milk
45 ml (3 T) grated cheese

1 Heat 45 ml (3 T) of the oil in a saucepan and fry the sweet potatoes until brown. Remove and keep warm.
2 In another saucepan, heat the remaining oil and fry the onions until they are soft. Add the mince and brown it.
3 Add the tomatoes, tomato paste, vinegar and seasoning. Cover and simmer for 30 minutes.
4 Grease a large ovenproof dish. Arrange layers of sweet potatoes and mince stew in it.
5 CHEESE SAUCE: Melt butter/margarine in a saucepan, add the flour and cook for 1 minute, stirring continuously. Add the milk and stir until thick. Remove from the heat and add the cheese.
6 Pour the sauce over the meat, sprinkle with breadcrumbs and bake at 180 °C (350 °F/gas 4) for 45 minutes.

STEWED NKWANI

PUMPKIN LEAVES

SERVES **4**
1 bunch pumpkin leaves
water
2 ml (½ t) bicarbonate of soda
salt and pepper to taste
1 onion, chopped
2 tomatoes, chopped

1 Rinse the pumpkin leaves thoroughly under running water and remove the strings. Slice thinly and place in a saucepan.
2 Cover the leaves with water, add bicarbonate of soda (to help retain the colour of the leaves), salt and pepper.
3 `bring to the boil and then add the onions and tomatoes. Reduce the heat and simmer for about 20 minutes, or until it is cooked.

KAPENTA YAIMPIKWA

FRESH KAPENTA

SERVES 4

500 ml (2 cups) kapenta

125 ml (½ cup) oil

2 large onions, chopped

3 tomatoes, peeled and chopped

10 ml (2 t) salt

3 ml (½ t) Aromat

1 Clean the kapenta with hot water. Heat the oil in a pan and fry the fish for about 10 minutes until brown.

2 Add the onions and tomatoes to the kapenta and mix well. Simmer gently for 5 minutes. Serve with porridge (for the Zambian equivalent of Malawi's *nsima, see* the recipe for *nshima* on page 84).

Kapenta is a tiny fish, popular in Zambia, Malawi and Zimbabwe. It is available fresh, but is mostly used in its dried form. This recipe can be used for both dry and fresh kapenta. If kapenta is not available, white-bait or any small white fish could be used instead.

MASAMBA CAKES

SPINACH CAKES

MAKES 8

1 bunch *masamba* (spinach), rinsed and chopped

110 g (4 oz)/250 ml (1 cup) cooked macaroni

2 eggs

100 g (4 oz)/500 ml (2 cups) fresh breadcrumbs

salt to taste

2 ml (½ t) sugar

60 g (2 oz)/125 ml (½ cup) cake flour

60 g (2 oz)/60 ml (4 T) butter/margarine

water

1 Place the spinach in a saucepan and cook until wilted. Chop finely.

2 Mix the cooked macaroni into the spinach, add 1 egg, half the breadcrumbs, salt and sugar.

3 Mix well and form into flat cakes.

4 Beat the second egg and mix it with the remaining breadcrumbs in a separate container. Coat the cakes in flour and then in the egg and breadcrumb mixture.

5 Heat the oil and fry the cakes until cooked through. Serve with a savoury sauce, such as tomato relish (*see* page 27).

MANDAZI

FAT CAKES

MAKES 24

480 g (17 oz)/4 x 250 ml (4 cups) cake flour

30 ml (2 T) baking powder

10 ml (2 t) cream of tartar

100 g (4 oz)/125 ml (½ cup) sugar

4 eggs, beaten

± 250 ml (1 cup) milk to mix

oil for deep frying

1 Sift together the flour, baking powder and cream of tartar.

2 Add the sugar and carefully mix in the eggs.

3 Add enough milk to form a stiff batter.

4 Heat the oil, drop spoonfuls of batter into the hot oil and deep-fry until brown on all sides.

5 Drain on kitchen paper and serve hot with tea.

VARIATIONS:

• Add 5 crushed cardamom seeds to the mixture before frying.

• Serve with a savoury mince filling or with jam.

STEWED CHAMBO

SERVES 6

30 ml (2 T) oil

2 onions, chopped

4 tomatoes, peeled and chopped

5 ml (1 t) turmeric

salt and pepper to taste

1 whole chambo of approximately
500 g (18 oz), or any other firm
white fish, cut into portions

1 Heat the oil in a saucepan and sauté the onions until they are transparent.

2 Add the tomatoes, turmeric, salt and pepper.

3 Simmer until thickened.

4 Add the chambo pieces, adding some water if the stew seems dry. Heat until boiling, cover the saucepan, reduce the heat and simmer for about 30 minutes, until the fish is cooked.

VARIATION: Dried chambo is steamed and served topped with the same sauce as described above, or brushed with oil and grilled. One dried chambo serves 4.

ZANZIBAR
TANZANIA

The exotic island of Zanzibar off the East African coast has ancient links with both Arabia and the mainland of Africa. The Arab influence on Zanzibar and Pemba islands is reflected in the inhabitants, a mixture of Shirazis (from ancient Persia), Arabs and Comorans (from the Comoros islands).

Zanzibar was initially granted independence in 1963, when power passed to the ruling class of the Sultan and Arabs. A violent revolution in January 1964, however, killed and sent into exile about a fifth of the Arab population, and power was eventually seized by the leader of the

Afro-Shiraz Party, Abeid Karume, who later became the first president of the Republic of Tanzania. Later that same year, Zanzibar finally became part of the United Republic of Tanzania – now the largest of the East African countries – when the newly independent territories of Tanganyika and Zanzibar merged into one nation.

Despite the union, however, Zanzibar remains somewhat isolated and separate. Although the Zanzibari people speak Swahili (kiswahili), they continue to embrace the Arab culture and Islamic faith. Zanzibar's food, then, incorporates a little Arabic cuisine, generous quantities of aromatic Indian spices, and a touch of Africa.

Zanzibar's prosperity was based largely on cloves grown on Arab-owned plantations and, for many years, it was the sole supplier of cloves – until other countries started growing the popular spice. This forced Zanzibar to look to tourism to boost its revenue and the spice tour – which includes visits to the spice plantations and a spice factory – is very popular. It is fascinating to watch young boys and men climb up a high tree to pick black pepper, and to see other spices like nutmeg, turmeric and cloves in their raw state.

I spent a day with Vulai Mwini and his family, practising Muslims who live just outside Stone Town. The women taught me how to roll pastry for samoosas and *chapatis*, while other typical dishes included *Kaimati* (grated coconut fritters), cassava in coconut sauce, and *tambi* (noodles in syrup). Coconut milk is used in many recipes, and is made by breaking a fresh coconut open and shredding the flesh, which is then mixed with cold water and squeezed through a strainer.

LEFT *A happy family outside their home.*
ABOVE *A young boy wearing a hat woven from palm leaves.*
OPPOSITE *Dhows glide across a calm sea.*

CHICKEN WITH MANGO SAUCE

Serves 6–8

1 whole chicken of 750g–1 kg (1½–2½ lb)

750 ml (3 cups) water

salt to taste

2 garlic cloves, crushed

1 onion, chopped

3 ml (½ t) cinnamon

5 ml (1 t) black pepper

250 ml (1 cup) coconut milk

2 green mangoes, sliced

SAUCE

250 ml (1 cup) coconut milk

45 ml (3 T) oil

250 ml (1 cup) mashed potatoes

salt to taste

10 ml (2 t) turmeric

Garnish

1 mango, sliced

1 onion, sliced

1 egg, hard-boiled and sliced

1 tomato, sliced

1 Cook the chicken in salted water with the garlic, onion, cinnamon, black pepper, coconut milk and green mango.

2 When the chicken has cooked through, remove the mango slices and prepare the sauce.

3 SAUCE: Boil together the coconut milk and oil. Add the mashed mango (from the chicken) and the mashed potatoes. Season with salt, turmeric and pepper. Moisten with stock from the cooked chicken.

4 TO SERVE: Place the chicken on a serving platter, pour the sauce over it and garnish with mango slices, sliced onions, sliced hard-boiled eggs and sliced tomatoes.

LOBSTER MAYONNAISE

Serves 1

1 lobster

250 ml (1 cup) water

juice of 1 lemon

salt and pepper to taste

1 onion, sliced

75 ml (5 T) mayonnaise

45 ml (3 T) water

freshly ground pepper to taste

1 Remove the flesh from the lobster. Heat the water to boiling point and add the lemon juice, salt, pepper, onion and lobster flesh. Simmer for 10 minutes.

2 Remove the lobster and keep warm. In the same water, boil the lobster shell for 5 minutes. Remove and rinse under cold water.

3 Place the shell on a serving dish. Slice the lobster flesh and spoon it into the shell.

4 Mix the mayonnaise with 45 ml (3 T) water and spread it on the lobster. Sprinkle with black pepper before serving.

FRIED OCTOPUS

SERVES 4
500 g (18 oz) octopus
water
30 g (1 oz)/30 ml (2 T) butter
30 ml (2 T) lemon juice
1 onion, chopped
1 garlic clove, chopped
15 ml (1 T) chopped ginger
2 green chillies, chopped
5 ml (1 t) cumin seeds
5 ml (1 t) turmeric

1 Cover the octopus with water and boil it for
20 minutes. Remove the octopus from the pot.
2 Meanwhile, in a large frying pan, melt the
butter and add all the remaining ingredients.
Sauté for about 10 minutes.
3 Add the octopus and stir-fry for 8 minutes.
Serve with a salad.

CHAPATIS

MAKES 8–10
240 g (9 oz)/500 ml (2 cups) cake flour
125 ml (½ cup) lukewarm water
125 ml (½ cup) coconut oil
45 ml (3 T) vegetable fat
45 ml (3 T) oil

1 DOUGH: Mix the flour with the lukewarm
water, coconut oil and vegetable fat. Knead
together until it makes a smooth, pliable dough.
Form into large balls and leave to rest for about
30 minutes.
2 Roll the dough out into a large circle. Stretch
it out and make a large hole in the centre. Tear
the dough to form it into a long strip, and form
the strip into tight circles. Cover and allow to
rest. Roll out again until thin and flat. Shallow-
fry the chapatis in hot oil on a griddle or heavy-
based frying pan.

ZANZIBAR MIX

SERVES 6–8
BHAJIYAS
200 g (7 oz)/250 ml (1 cup) lentils
125 ml (½ cup) oil
salt to taste

SAUCE
250 ml (1 cup) water
45 ml (3 T) flour
10 ml (2 t) turmeric
salt to taste
1 mango, peeled and diced

POTATOES
2 potatoes
2 green bananas

CASSAVA CRISPS
2 cassava
250 ml (1 cup) oil
10 ml (2 t) chilli powder

RED OR GREEN CHUTNEY
12 red or green chillies
salt to taste
1 lime or ½ lemon
1 green mango

COCONUT CHUTNEY
125 ml (½ cup) grated coconut
salt to taste
1 red chilli, finely chopped
1 green mango, cut into pieces
1 lemon, cut into pieces
30 ml (2 T) sugar

LENTILS

200 g (7 oz)/250 ml (1 cup) gram lentils

500 ml (2 cups) water

salt to taste

GARNISH

ground nuts

1 BHAJIYAS: Soak the lentils overnight, drain and purée until smooth. Form the lentil purée into balls and deep-fry. Season with salt.

2 SAUCE: Heat the water to boiling point in a saucepan. Mix the flour with a little cold water to form a paste. Add the turmeric, salt and flour paste to the saucepan. Add the raw mango pieces and mix through. Cook for 1 minute.

3 POTATOES: Boil the potatoes until cooked, peel and cut into quarters. In another saucepan, boil the green bananas for 10 minutes. Slice the bananas and mix with the potatoes.

4 CASSAVA CRISPS: Peel the raw cassava and slice into sticks. Deep-fry in hot oil, season with salt and chilli powder.

5 RED OR GREEN CHUTNEY: Cut the chillies through the middle, remove the seeds and place the chillies in a liquidiser. Add salt, small pieces of lemon or lime and green mango.

6 COCONUT CHUTNEY: Mix together the grated coconut, salt, red chillies, green mango and lemon. Season with the sugar.

7 LENTILS: Soak the lentils overnight in salted water and boil for about 20 minutes until soft. Drain if all the water has not been absorbed.

8 TO ASSEMBLE: Place the potatoes in a bowl. Add the lentils and the sauce. Mix everything together. Cut the *bhajiyas* in half and put them on top, with the coconut chutney and the red or green chutney. Add the cassava crisps. Sprinkle with ground nuts and serve hot with chutneys.

VARIATION: The cassava crisps can be replaced with potato crisps.

KAIMATI

Serves 4–6

500 g (18 oz)/4 x 250 ml (4 cups) cake flour

1 packet (10 g) instant yeast

250 ml (1 cup) lukewarm milk

30 g (1 oz)/30 ml (2 T) butter

250 ml (1 cup) coconut milk

SYRUP

500 ml (2 cups) water

200 g (7 oz)/250 ml (1 cup) sugar

15 ml (1 T) ground cinnamon

1 Mix together the flour and yeast. Mix the lukewarm milk with the butter, add to the flour and knead to mix.

2 Gradually add the coconut milk. Mix until the dough is smooth and pliable. Leave in a warm place until double in size.

3 Heat the oil and form the dough into balls the size of golf balls. Deep-fry until cooked through.

4 SYRUP: Boil all the ingredients together.

5 Dip the kaimati into the syrup and allow to cool. Serve as a desert or with coffee or tea.

VIPOPOO

Makes ± 24

120 g (4½ oz)/250 ml (1 cup) cake flour

62,5 ml (¼ cup) each water and coconut milk

45 ml (3 T) sugar

10 ml (2 t) ground cardamom

1 Mix together the cake flour and water until smooth. Roll into balls the size of small marbles.

2 Boil together the coconut milk, sugar and ground cardamom.

3 Add the pastry balls to the coconut milk and cook for 5 minutes. Serve as dessert.

CURRIED PLANTAINS

Serves 4

4 plantains, peeled

25 ml (2 T) corn oil or butter

2 onions, chopped

4 garlic cloves, crushed

2 tomatoes, chopped

5 ml (1 t) turmeric

salt and pepper to taste

250 ml (1 cup) coconut milk

1 Cover plantains with water; boil 20 minutes.

2 Heat the oil or butter and sauté the onions and garlic until transparent.

3 Add the tomatoes, turmeric, salt and pepper and mix well. Gently add the plantains.

4 In a small saucepan, heat the coconut milk to boiling point, then reduce the heat and cook gently for 10–15 minutes. Stir the coconut milk into the curried plantains. Serve with grilled fish or meat or over rice.

VISHETI

MAKES ± 24

DOUGH

120 g (4½ oz)/250 ml (1 cup) cake flour

75 ml (⅓ cup) lukewarm water

62,5 ml (¼ cup) coconut oil

62,5 ml (¼ cup) vegetable fat

SUGAR SYRUP

250 ml (1 cup) water

50 g (2 oz)/62,5 ml (¼ cup) sugar

5 ml (1 t) vanilla essence

3 ml (½ t) ground cardamom

1 DOUGH: Mix the flour with the lukewarm water, coconut oil and vegetable fat. Knead together until it makes a smooth, pliable dough. Form into balls the size of large marbles and leave to rest for about 30 minutes.

2 Roll the dough into a long, thin, cylindrical shape. Cut into small pieces. Leave to rest for 10 minutes.

3 SUGAR SYRUP: Mix the water with the sugar, vanilla essence and ground cardamom.

4 Deep-fry the dough in hot oil. Remove from the oil and drain.

5 Coat with sugar syrup. Serve with coffee.

TAMBI

SERVES 6–8

500 g (18 oz) tambi

750 ml (3 cups) water

salt

75 ml (5 T) sugar

45 ml (3 T) oil

6 cardamom seeds, crushed

1 Cook the tambi in boiling salted water for about 10 minutes until soft. Drain.

2 Sprinkle the tambi with sugar and oil, season with cardamom, mix through and serve.

CASSAVA AND CHANGU WITH COCONUT SAUCE

SERVES 6–8

2 cassava, peeled and boiled

125 ml (½ cup) coconut milk

1 whole changu

1 Cook the cassava in the coconut milk for about 20 minutes until it is soft.

2 Place the fish on top of the cassava and gently cook for about 30 minutes, until the flavours are well blended.

> Changu can be replaced with any medium-sized firm white fish, such as hake.

KENYA

Kenya remains, for many people, the epitome of Africa, and nowhere is this image more evident than the abundance of its wildlife, most notably in the famed Masai Mara National Reserve. Every year, millions of wildebeest migrate south, as do large numbers of pink flamingoes, and neighbouring Tanzania's Mount Kilimanjaro provides the perfect backdrop for elephant crossing the plains.

The capital city, Nairobi, is bustling, friendly and the heart of the relatively prosperous country. Mombasa, steeped in a rich Arab history, is the largest port on the coast of East Africa and serves many neighbouring states.

Prior to colonialism, there were no pre-existing kingdoms uniting the individual African societies. Although the Sultan of Zanzibar

exercised some control over Arab-dominated cities along the coast – Lamu, Malindi and Mombasa – he had little influence over the indigenous people of the interior.

Kenya is home to almost every major language group of Africa, including the 'click' language of the San and Khoi, but the official languages are Swahili (kiswahili) and English. With a population of nearly 30 million, the main indigenous groups comprise the Kikuyu, Kamba, Luhya and Maasai, but it is the Maasai, more than any other group that has come to symbolise traditional Kenya.

My host family in Mombasa was Mama-Omodi and her daughters, Scolastica, Ambi, Kamene and Pola. They all enthusiastically showed me how to prepare family meals Mombasa-style. Mama-Omodi and her daughters all participate in cooking the main meal of the day, and they occasionally break into song.

The open-air kitchen teems with life and the smell of food cooking on the *jiko* (charcoal burner) is inviting. Mama-Omodi occasionally dips into the dark recesses of her bosom to buy more ingredients while supervising the cooking.

The daughters take turns to break and grate the coconut, which is then placed in a wet *kifumbu* (conical basket) and squeezed to produce coconut milk. The spices are ground in an over-used pestle and mortar, and the tomatoes crushed in a modern blender. Great care is taken when cleaning and gutting fish, and also in chopping and peeling fresh vegetables. Then the seasoning is checked, and the meal is finished off and garnished.

I encountered an unusual method of cooking rice, unique to Mombasa. The rice is placed in a saucepan with water and then covered with a newspaper. Hot coals are then placed on a tray on top of the paper. The rice then simmers slowly under the hot coals. After cooking, the dry coat on top of the rice is gently removed so that it comes off in one piece.

LEFT *Young Maasai girls showing their colourful beadwork.*
ABOVE *Samburu men dancing.*
OPPOSITE *Graceful oryx grazing in the tranquil bush.*

UGALI CAKE AND SUKUMA WIKI WITH ZEBRA AND TOMATO CONCASSE

SERVES 4

± 1 litre (4 cups) water

360 g (12 oz)/750 ml (3 cups) *ugali* (maize-meal)

30 g (1 oz)/30 ml (2 T) butter/margarine

200 g (7 oz) *sukuma wiki*

2 onions, finely chopped

1 garlic clove, crushed

salt and pepper to taste

30 ml (2 T) oil

500 g (18 oz) zebra steak, cut into serving portions

½ x 410 g (14 oz) can tomato concasse or salsa

1 carrot, cut into strips

1 brinjal, cut into strips

1 Boil the water in a saucepan and then add the maize-meal. Cook, stirring continuously, until the porridge is stiff.

2 Melt butter/margarine and fry the *sukuma wiki*, onions and garlic for 3 minutes. Season.

3 Heat the oil and pan-fry the zebra steaks. Remove the steaks from the pan.

4 Add 15 ml (1 T) oil to the pan and fry the brinjal and carrot strips.

5 Arrange the steaks on a warm plate with the *ugali* and *sukuma wiki*. Garnish with concasse or salsa and top with fried strips of carrots and brinjal.

> *Ugali* is the local porridge.
> *Sukuma wiki*, loosely translated, means 'push the week'. It is a type of wild leaf on which most homes rely when money is scarce. Spinach can be used as a substitute.

BEEF STEW

SERVES 4–6

30 ml (2 T) oil

500 g (18 oz) beef, cubed

6 tomatoes, grated

250 ml (1 cup) coconut milk

15 ml (1 T) chopped dhania

1 chilli, chopped

salt to taste

1 Heat the oil in a saucepan and brown the beef.

2 Add the remaining ingredients and simmer for about 45 minutes, until the meat is cooked.

MATAHA

PEA, CORN AND POTATO MASH

SERVES 4–6

500 ml (2 cups) shelled garden peas

500 ml (2 cups) corn from the cob

5 potatoes

30 ml (2 T) oil

salt to taste

1 Cook vegetables separately. Mash potatoes. Heat oil and add all the ingredients.

3 Heat through and mix until all the ingredients are mashed together.

PILAU

SERVES 4–6

30 ml (2 T) oil

500 g (18 oz) beef, cubed

15 ml (1 T) mixed spices

250 ml (1 cup) beef stock

150 g (5 oz) peas

4 carrots, diced

200 g (7 oz)/250 ml (1 cup) uncooked rice

1 Heat the oil in a saucepan and brown the beef with the spices.

2 Add the stock to the saucepan and cook until the meat is tender.

3 Add the peas, carrots and rice, toss together and cook for a further 15 minutes. Serve with *kachumbari* (tomato, onion and vinegar salad).

> Pilau is a popular dish at weddings and other large gatherings. Spices like chillies, garlic, dhania, curry powder and turmeric are crushed together to produce the desired flavour.

FISH STEW

SERVES 6–8

2 red onions, chopped

1 garlic clove, crushed

4 tomatoes, peeled and diced

2 chillies, chopped

45 ml (3 T) ground coriander

15 ml (1 T) curry powder

5 ml (1 t) turmeric

250 ml (1 cup) oil

2 whole tafi, cod or kabeljou, or equivalent small fish, of approximately 250 g (9 oz) each

1 tin (75 g/3 oz) tomato paste

250 ml (1 cup) coconut milk

15 ml (1 T) dhania leaves

1 Place the onions, garlic and tomatoes in a blender and purée until smooth.

2 Mix the chillies, coriander, curry and turmeric, and grind the mixed spices. Cut deep slits into the fish and rub the fish with the mixed spices, pressing well into the slits.

3 Heat the oil and deep-fry the fish.

4 Remove the fish and place it in a saucepan. Add the tomato purée, tomato paste, coconut milk and chopped dhania leaves.

5 Bring to the boil and then simmer for about 10 minutes. Garnish with dhania leaves.

SKEWERED IRIO BALLS WITH BARRACUDA IN COCONUT SAUCE

SERVES 4

200 g (7 oz) potatoes, peeled and boiled

100 g (4 oz) frozen peas, cooked

200 g (7 oz) *sukuma wiki*, cooked

½ tin (410 g/14 oz) creamed sweet corn

salt and pepper to taste

125 ml (½ cup) flour

oli for frying

50 ml (3 T) oil

500 g (18 oz) barracuda

2 onions, chopped

1 garlic clove, crushed

30 ml (2 T) chopped dhania

3 ml (½ t) turmeric

200 ml (1 cup) coconut milk

1 Mash potatoes, peas, *sukuma wiki* and sweet corn. Form into balls the size of golf balls, roll in flour and deep-fry in hot oil. Thread onto 4 skewers.

2 Heat 15 ml (1 T) oil and pan-fry fish. Remove from pan and keep warm. Add remaining oil to pan and sauté onions, garlic and dhania until soft.

3 Add the turmeric and coconut milk and cook for 3 minutes.

4 Place the skewered vegetables on a warm plate. Arrange the fried fish, pour sauce around the fish and serve immediately.

BRINJAL STEW

Serves 4–6
4 brinjals, peeled
45 ml (3 T) oil
1 onion, sliced
10 ml (2 t) curry powder
250 ml (1 cup) coconut milk
salt

1 Slice the brinjals lengthways, but do not cut right through.
2 Heat the oil and fry the onion with the curry powder until soft.
3 Add the coconut milk and heat until it boils.
4 Add the brinjals, season and allow to simmer for about 20 minutes until cooked.

GRILLED CHANGU

Serves 6–8
1 whole changu, cod or kabeljou
oil for basting
salt and pepper to taste

1 Grill the fish on both sides for 30 minutes, or until cooked. Serve with rice.
VARIATION: Grill the fish for 15 minutes only. Bring 250 ml (1 cup) coconut milk to the boil in a saucepan, add the grilled fish and cook for another 15 minutes.

MUCHICHA AND PEAS

Serves 4
1 bunch of muchicha, washed and steamed
250 ml (1 cup) peas
4 tomatoes, grated
2 red onions, chopped
250 ml (1 cup) coconut milk

1 Rinse the muchicha and peas. Steam together until soft.
2 Add the tomatoes, onions and coconut milk. Mix to blend.
3 Simmer gently for about 20 minutes until cooked through. Serve with porridge (*see* the recipe for *nshima* on page 84 for the Zambian equivalent of Kenya's *ugali*).

GHANA

As early as the thirteenth century, a number of kingdoms were established in Ghana – and each had a strong culture of trading. The best known and most powerful of these nations was the Ashanti kingdom, which by the late seventeenth century had conquered most of the other groups.

The Ashanti capital of Kumasi was highly efficient, with facilities and services equal to most European capitals at the time – but all this came to rather abrupt end with the beginning of the slave trade to the Americas in the 1800s.

The modern state of Ghana extends from the Gulf of Guinea and stretches approximately 640 kilometres inland. Most of the countryside consists largely of wooded hills and wide valleys, with a low-lying coastal plain.

Ghana gained its independence from Britain in 1957, but many of its 18-million-strong population speak English, and it is the country's official language, with the main African languages Akan, Twi, Fante, Ga, Ewe, Dagbeni, Hausa and Nzima. Although most Ghanaians are Christian, many still follow traditional beliefs and there is a minority of Muslims.

The capital of Ghana is the lively Accra, and the vibrant lifestyle, colourfully dressed Ghanaians – the kente cloth has its origins here – and buzzing city centre make Accra a truly African metropolis.

A lot of food is sold on the streets. Rice with spicy chicken or fish stew is wrapped artistically in banana leaves, and plantains – a type of banana – are roasted on open fires and sold by street vendors. Women, carrying large dishes of vegetables and fruit on their heads in true African style, walk up and down the streets, selling their wares.

Mercy Debrah welcomed us into her home-cum-restaurant, and I watched in awe as the food was prepared. A muscular Joe Otongo pounded boiled cassava into a pulp using a pestle and mortar, after which it was pureed until smooth and then rolled to make *fufu*. Ghanaian food has a distinct flavour: most dishes are delicately spiced with chillies, garlic, palm oil and peanut sauce. I enjoyed the crumbly but moist *gari foto* and the 'light soups' made with tilapia fish or goats' milk, which are served with the tangy *kenkey*, sticky *fufu*, or the robust *banku*.

LEFT *A crab-seller shows his wares.*
ABOVE *Smiling Ghanaian woman.*
OPPOSITE *Traditional fishing boat on the beach at Elmina.*

3 Add the tuna, carrots and green pepper and allow to simmer until soft.

4 Beat 3 eggs and boil 1 until hard. Slowly stir the beaten egg into the sauce.

5 Sprinkle water lightly on the gari and gently mix the sauce into the gari. Check the seasoning.

6 Garnish a serving platter with lettuce leaves and spoon the gari foto on the lettuce. Garnish with the boiled egg, cut into wedges.

GARI FOTO

Serves 4–6

75 ml (5 T) soya oil

2 onions, sliced

15 ml (1 T) chilli pepper

4 tomatoes, chopped

30 ml (2 T) tomato paste

1 tin (175 g/6 oz) tuna, drained

2 carrots, diced

1 green pepper, diced

4 eggs

30 ml (2 T) water

250 ml (1 cup) gari

lettuce leaves

1 Heat the oil, add the onions and chilli pepper and sauté until soft.

2 Add the tomatoes and tomato paste to the onions. Stew for 15 minutes.

> *Gari* is made of dried and ground cassava. It can be replaced with cooked *phutu* (*see* the recipe on page 30) or maize-rice.

OKRA STEW WITH BANKU

Serves 4

500 g (18 oz) fish or goat meat

250 ml (1 cup) water

1 onion, sliced

45 ml (3 T) palm oil

2 tomatoes, chopped

1 green or yellow pepper, sliced

100 g (4 oz) kapenta or anchovies

250 ml (1 cup) okra, chopped

1 brinjal, chopped

125 ml (½ cup) wele (optional)

1 Cook the fish or goat meat in a little water until tender – approximately 20 minutes in the case of fish, and 1 hour for goat.

2 Fry the onion in palm oil until soft.

3 Add the chopped tomatoes, green or yellow peppers and kapenta or anchovies. Simmer for 5 minutes.

4 Add the okra and brinjal.

5 Mix in the cooked fish or meat and bring to the boil. If prefered, add wele (cow skin) for added flavour. Cook until the fish or meat is soft.

> The *kapenta* or anchovies used in this recipe can be replaced with any small salted fish.

BEEF PALAVA SAUCE

SERVES 6

500 g (18 oz) boneless beef, cut into cubes

1 onion, sliced

1 garlic clove, crushed

15 ml (1 T) crushed ginger

salt to taste

75 ml (5 T) palm oil

30 ml (2 T) tomato paste

2 chillies, chopped

2 tomatoes, chopped

2 carrots, diced

15 ml (1 T) *agushi* powder or 2 eggs, beaten

½ bunch spinach, washed and shredded

1 Steam the beef with half the onion, garlic, ginger and salt until soft. Set aside.

2 In another saucepan, heat the oil and sauté the remaining onions, garlic and ginger.

3 Add the tomato paste. Blend the chillies and tomatoes and add. Add the cooked beef and carrots. Simmer for 15 minutes.

4 Add the *agushi* or beaten egg and stir gently.

5 Add the spinach. Cook just a few minutes so that it retains its colour. Check the seasoning and serve with boiled ripe plantains or yams.

> *Agushi* is ground melon seed used for thickening.

CHICKEN AND PEANUT STEW

SERVES 4–6

125 ml (½ cup) peanut butter

30 ml (2 T) tomato paste

60 ml (½ cup) water

30 ml (2 T) palm oil

½ chicken, cut into portions

1 onion, chopped

1 garlic clove, crushed

30 ml (2 T) crushed ginger

3 chillies, crushed

3 tomatoes

2 chicken stock cubes dissolved in:

500 ml (2 cups) hot water

bay leaf and salt to taste

1 Mix the peanut butter with the tomato paste and the water. Cook the mixture until oil appears on top. Set aside.

2 Heat the oil and brown the chicken. Add the onion, garlic, ginger, chillies and tomatoes. Sauté together for 10 minutes.

3 Add peanut sauce and stock to the chicken. Season. Bring to the boil and then simmer gently for 45 minutes. Serve on rice.

KENKEY

Serves 6

500 ml (2 cups) raw maize kernels

water

salt to taste

banana leaves

GOAT MEAT LIGHT SOUP WITH FUFU

Serves 4–6

1 kg (2½ lb) goat meat

1 onion, finely chopped

15 ml (1 T) crushed ginger

salt to taste

1,25 litres (5 cups) water

2 ml (½ t) cayenne pepper

2 tomatoes, chopped

1 brinjal, peeled and chopped

125 ml (½ cup) canned butter or lima beans

(optional)

4 *fufu* balls

1 Season the goat meat with the finely chopped onion, crushed ginger and salt. Add 250 ml (1 cup) of the water to moisten and cook the meat gently in a saucepan for 30 minutes, stirring occasionally.

2 Add 1 litre (4 cups) water to the meat and heat until boiling.

3 Add cayenne pepper, tomatoes and brinjal. Cover and cook for 15 minutes. If prefered, add canned butter or lima beans.

4 Continue cooking for about 30 minutes, until the soup is well blended and the meat falls off the bones.

5 Place the *fufu* balls in the soup bowl and spoon the soup over.

1 Cover the maize with water and soak for three days. Rinse the maize and pound it to a pulp or blend until smooth.

2 Bind with a little water to form a thick dough. Allow to stand for another day to ferment.

3 Divide the dough into three parts. Cook two parts, softened with water, in a heavy pot for 30 minutes, stirring. Remove from the heat and mix with rest of the raw dough. Add salt.

4 Mould the *kenkey* into tennis ball shapes and wrap tightly with enough banana leaves to cover them completely. Line the pot with banana leaves and place the *kenkey* balls on the leaves.

5 Top with water and cook for 3 hours. Serve with meat or fish.

CHARCOAL-GRILLED RED SNAPPER

1 whole snapper, approximately 500 g (18 oz)

15 ml (1 T) chilli powder

15 ml (1 T) crushed ginger

1 garlic clove, crushed

3 tomatoes, sliced

1 onion, sliced

1 green pepper, sliced

salt to taste

OIL TO BASTE FISH

45 ml (3 T) soya oil

15 ml (1 T) each crushed garlic and ginger

1 bay leaf

3 ml (½ t) aniseed

salt to taste

1 SAUCE: Blend the chilli, ginger and garlic with a little of the sliced tomatoes and onions and use this as the base for the sauce.

2 OIL FOR BASTING: Blend all the ingredients.

3 Score the fish on both sides and baste it with the oil mixture. Grill for 20 minutes.

4 Pour the blended chilli mixture on a serving platter. Top with the grilled fish.

5 Mix remaining onion and tomato with green pepper, and spread the mixture on top of the fish. Serve with *kenkey* (*see* the recipe on p.114).

TILAPIA LIGHT SOUP AND BANKU

Serves 4–6

1 whole tilapia

1 large onion, chopped

2 large tomatoes, chopped

1 yellow pepper, sliced

1 brinjal, peeled and chopped

45 ml (3 T) palm oil

500 ml (2 cups) chicken stock

1 Scale and gut the tilapia.

2 Make a stew by frying the onion, tomatoes, yellow pepper and brinjal in the palm oil until the vegetables are soft.

3 Add the chicken stock and tilapia.

4 Cook gently for about 20 minutes until the fish is cooked through and flaky.

If tilapia is not available, it can be replaced with any firm-fleshed white fish.

Banku is a type of dumpling made with cassava flour (*gari*) or corn meal, and steamed in the stew. The preparation method is similar to that of wholewheat dumplings (*see* the recipe for *idombolo* on page 52).

COCONUT OR PEANUT BISCUITS

Makes 12

250 ml (1 cup) sugar

300 g (10 oz)/750 ml (3 cups) peanuts or

240 g (9 oz)/750 ml (3 cups) desiccated coconut

30 ml (2 T) glucose syrup

60 ml (4 T) water

1 Caramellise the sugar by heating it over a low heat until it has melted.

2 Add the peanuts or coconut and stir to blend.

3 Rub a table top or chopping board with butter and pour the mixture on to it.

4 Roll the mixture out with a rolling pin and cut into attractive shapes. Leave to dry and serve as dessert.

SENEGAL

Senegal nestles comfortably in the western extreme of the African continent, bound by Mauritania to the north, Mali to the east, Guinea and Guinea-Bissau to the south – and the Atlantic Ocean to the west.

Senegal was an early participant in the Atlantic slave trade. Ile de Goree – 16 hectares of arid land less than 10 kilometres from the mainland and one of the first French settlements in Africa – still bears evidence of the horrors of this trade. Still standing on the island is a museum dedicated to the slaves, old slave houses and colonial mansions. Few places on earth arouse as much emotion as Goree. The capital, Dakar, is a large modern city, and a major West African port, home to about an eighth of Senegal's population of 8.5 million. Although the country has around 20 ethnic groups – including the Wolofs, Fulani and the Serer – the people of Senegal enjoy a harmonious relationship, intermarrying freely.

Senegal has strong French ties. In 1946, French citizenship was extended to all Senegalese and, although the country eventually gained independence in 1974, French remains the official language. Artistic expression is rich and varied, but Senegal is best known for its musicians and, perhaps most significantly, the drum, a key element of local music.

Thiebou djeun, pronounced 'cheebo-oo-jenn', is the country's national dish, and Senegalese all over the world make a point of preparing this dish to remind them of home. The ingredients are easily accessible: *thiebou djeun* can range from a simple bowl of rice and vegetables to more exotic additions like fish. To honour guests, the Senegalese will serve *poulet yassa*, a lemon-marinated onion and chicken dish.

As in most of Africa, peanuts play an important role in local food. *Mafe* is a peanut sauce-based stew made with chicken, beef or mutton, and considered one of Senegal's culinary pillars. Traditionally, food is cooked on charcoal burners to ensure that it cooks slowly and that the flavours blend to perfection. After a meal, a sweet, minty green tea is served as a digestive – and you will inevitably drink three rounds: 'The first cup is bitter as death; the second as sweet as life; the third as mild as love.' It is also an art unto itself to pour this tea. The tiny tea pot is held high and the steaming hot tea gently falls in to the tiny glasses in which it is served.

LEFT *Interesting and artistic wooden carvings.*
ABOVE *These colourful buses are seen throughout Senegal.*
OPPOSITE *A fresh fruit and vegetable market.*

MAFFÉ D'AGREOU

LAMB WITH PEANUT
AND OKRA SAUCE

SERVES 4–6

45 ml (3 T) oil

500 g (18 oz) lamb, cut into cubes

2 onions, chopped

2 tomatoes, peeled and chopped

75 g (5 T) tomato paste

100 g (4 oz) peanut butter

2 sweet potatoes, peeled and quartered

100 g (3 oz) fresh okra, trimmed and chopped

1 large cassava, peeled and chopped

1 red pepper, chopped

salt and pepper to taste

500 ml (2 cups) water

POULET YASSA

CHICKEN
IN ONION SAUCE

SERVES 4–6

4 onions, sliced

125 ml (½ cup) lemon juice

salt and black pepper to taste

3 ml (½ t) cayenne pepper

45 ml (3 T) oil

1 large chicken, cut into portions

45 ml (3 T) mustard

1 Mix together the onions, lemon juice and seasoning. Leave to stand for 30 minutes.

2 Heat the oil and fry the onions gently until transparent.

3 Meanwhile, coat the chicken pieces with mustard, salt and pepper. Marinate 15 minutes.

4 Deep-fry or oven-roast the chicken portions until brown and cooked through.

5 Add the chicken to the onion sauce. Cook gently to blend the flavours, the longer the better. Moisten with water if it gets dry. Serve hot on cooked rice.

1 Heat the oil and brown the lamb. Remove it from the pot and keep it warm.

2 Add the onion to the pot and sauté until transparent. Add all the remaining ingredients, except the water, and stir-fry for about 5 minutes.

3 Add the water, return the lamb to the pot and simmer, covered, for about 50–60 minutes. Serve on rice.

THIOF FARCI À LA SAINT LOUISIEN

STUFFED FISH IN VEGETABLE STEW

SERVES 6–8

1 whole thiof of approximately 500 g (18 oz)

STUFFING

500 g (18 oz) fish steaks, filleted

500 ml (2 cups) breadcrumbs

SAUCE

45 ml (3 T) peanut oil

1 onion, chopped

1 garlic clove, crushed

1 red pepper, chopped

1 bouquet garni (2–3 sprigs of parsley,

1 sprig of thyme and 1–2 bay leaves)

1 tin (115 g/4 oz) tomato paste

4 ripe tomatoes, pulped

500 ml (2 cups) water

VEGETABLES

1 carrot, peeled and coarsely chopped

1 leek, coarsely chopped

1 red pepper, cut into large pieces

100 g (4 oz) cabbage, cut into large pieces

1 brinjal, quartered

3 potatoes, peeled and quartered

salt and pepper to taste

1 Clean and gut the fish.

2 STUFFING: Purée the fish steaks and bread-crumbs in a blender.

3 Stuff the fish and place it in a large oven dish.

4 SAUCE: Heat the oil and sauté the onion, garlic and red pepper until soft. Add the bouquet garni, tomato paste, tomatoes and water.

5 Pour the sauce over the fish. Place all the prepared vegetables around the fish.

6 Cover and bake at 180 °C (350 °F/gas 4) for 45 minutes. Serve with rice.

Thiof may be substituted with any firm white fish.

THIEBOU DJEUN

FISH STEW WITH MIXED VEGETABLES

SERVES 6–8

1 kg (2½ lb) whole thiof, or any
firm-fleshed white fish

1 onion, grated

1 garlic clove, crushed

30 ml (2 T) chopped parsley

2 chillies, chopped

60 ml (4 T) oil

125 ml (½ cup) tomato purée

4 tomatoes, peeled and chopped

½ cabbage, cut into large chunks

4 carrots, peeled and cut in half

2 brinjals, quartered

4 x 250 ml (4 cups) water

salt and pepper to taste

500 ml (2 cups) rice

1 Cut deep slits in the fish. Mix the onion, garlic, parsley and chillies to a paste. Rub this paste into the slits. Allow to stand for at least 1 hour.

2 Cut the fish into big chunks. Heat the oil and deep-fry the fish until brown.

3 Place the tomato purée, tomatoes, vegetables and water in a saucepan and cook until soft. Season with salt and pepper.

4 Add the fish to the vegetable stew and cook for 10 minutes.

5 Remove fish and vegetables with a slotted spoon and keep warm in oven. Use the sauce to cook the rice, adding more water if necessary, depending how much rice is used. Check the seasoning. Cook the rice about 30 minutes.

6 Spread the rice on a large platter. Arrange the fish and vegetables on top.

This is Senegal's national dish. Local fish, such as meruo or thiof, is used and it is served on short-grain rice.

These pastry snacks are served as a light meal or starter, with a chilli tomato sauce.

PASTELLE

MAKES ±12
DOUGH
120 g (4½ oz)/250 ml (1 cup) flour
salt to taste
1 egg, beaten
water
15 ml (1 T) oil

FILLING
1 onion, grated
30 ml (2 T) chopped parsley
1 garlic clove, crushed
250 ml (1 cup) cooked white fish
salt and pepper to taste

1 Mix together the flour, salt, egg and enough water to form a stiff dough. Pour the oil over the dough and leave to soak for 30 minutes.
2 Knead the dough again, incorporating the oil. Roll out thinly and cut first into strips and then into squares.
3 FILLING: Combine all the ingredients and purée in a blender until smooth.
4 Place a teaspoon of filling on each pastry square, seal tightly and deep-fry in hot oil.

SOUPIKANDIA RIZ À LA SAUCE GOMBO

SEAFOOD AND OKRA STEW ON RICE

SERVES 4
125 ml (½ cup) palm oil
1 onion, chopped
500 g (18 oz) white fish, filleted and diced
250 g (9 oz) fresh okra, trimmed and chopped
2 red peppers, chopped

50 g (2 oz) dried fish, finely chopped
salt and pepper to taste
10 ml (2 t) chopped parsley
250 g (9 oz) shrimps or oysters (optional)
500 ml (2 cups) water

1 Heat the oil, add the chopped onion and sauté until transparent.
2 Add all the remaining ingredients. Simmer gently for 45 minutes until the fish is cooked through and the vegetables are soft.
3 Garnish with cooked whole okra and pepper. Serve with rice.

MOROCCO

Morocco is indeed a land of contrasts. Moulded by its many different people and demarcated by stark geographical features, such as the Rif and Atlas mountains that form its backbone, the country borders both the Atlantic and Mediterranean coasts, proudly occupying the northwest corner of Africa.

Morocco is characterised by desert sands and thick forests, the rocky Atlas and fertile plains, desert and mountain, and beyond lies the outer fringe of the Sahara. Its cities, such as Casablanca, Marrakesh, Fes and the capital at Rabat, teem with life and people, ranging from the traditional

Berber-speaking mountain peasants to the urbane, French-speaking upper echelons.

The French and Spanish restored Morocco's independence in 1956, and, as one of Africa's three monarchies, the country has since been ruled by Muhammad V and his son Hassan II.

The majority of Morocco's population of nearly 28 million are Sunni Muslims, and the official languages are Arabic, French, Spanish and English.

North African food – exotic, colourful and rich with the flavours of warm spices – has become increasingly popular throughout the world. The staple grain, *couscous*, is always accompanied by spicy stews called *tajines*, aromatic chicken, lamb or beef dishes generously flavoured with saffron and olives. Moroccan *mezes* are mostly purées, dips, marinated olives and cooked or raw vegetables. For a typical meal, one can serve a selection of *mezes* as a first course, accompanied by bread, and then leave them on the table throughout the meal.

Characteristic of Moroccan cuisine are the pastries made from wafer-thin *warka*, rich desserts and the popular mint tea, which locals

fondly refer to as 'Moroccan whisky'. Moroccan cuisine has its roots in several ancient cultures. The succession of different peoples who have invaded, traded with or visited North Africa over the centuries have all left their legacies. The diet of the nomadic Berbers and Bedouins is still evident today: *smen* (a cooked and aged butter), dates and grains (such as *couscous*) may be attributed to these groups. The Mediterranean influence is, of course, also apparent in the *mezes* served as the first course.

LEFT *Ceramic pots displayed on the roadside.*
ABOVE *A Moroccan waiter with many mouth-watering dishes.*
OPPOSITE *A village in the Atlas mountains.*

B'STILLA

CHICKEN OR PIGEON PIE

SERVES 8

1 medium chicken, jointed, or 2 young pigeons

2 onions, grated

3 ml (½ t) saffron

3 ml (½ t) ground cinnamon

90 ml (6 T) oil

salt and pepper to taste

1 bunch fresh coriander, chopped

1 bunch fresh parsley, chopped

8 eggs, beaten

10 sheets phyllo pastry

100 g (4 oz)/250 ml (1 cup) blanched almonds, coarsely chopped and toasted

20 ml (4 t) ground cinnamon for sprinkling (optional)

60 ml (4 T) icing sugar for sprinkling (optional)

1 Put the chicken or pigeons in a large saucepan. Add the onions, ginger, saffron, 3 ml (½ t) of the cinnamon, 45 ml (3 T) of the oil and sessoning. Add a little water – the birds must be braised, not boiled. Cover and cook gently, turning occasionally until tender.

2 Remove the chicken or pigeons and leave to cool. Discard the skin and bones. Add the coriander and parsley to the pan and boil, uncovered, until reduced to a thick sauce.

3 Over a low heat, gently stir in the eggs and scramble them. Remove from heat.

4 Pre-heat the oven to 190 °C (375 °F/gas 5). Thoroughly oil a metal baking tin about 32 cm (13 in) in diameter and 5 cm (2 in) deep. Lay a sheet of phyllo pastry in the tin, allowing the loose edges to fall over the sides. Brush with oil. Repeat with four more sheets, brushing with oil, so that the tin is completely covered.

5 Cover with the chicken or pigeon pieces, then the egg mixture. Cover with a small sheet of phyllo pastry and scatter over the almonds. Sprinkle with 10 ml (2 t) cinnamon and 30 ml (2 T) of the icing sugar, if prefered.

6 Fold the overhanging edges of the pastry over the almonds. Cover with the remaining pastry, brushing each sheet with oil. Tuck the edges inside the tin and under the pie.

7 Bake for about 45 minutes until crisp and golden. If prefered, sieve 30 ml (2 T) icing sugar over the top and make a lattice pattern with the remaining 10 ml (2 t) ground cinnamon. Serve hot with a salad.

> B'stilla is one of the great dishes of North Africa. It is served hot as a first course, and is best eaten using the fingers. In Morocco the crust is made of tissue-thin warka, for which phyllo pastry is the most practical substitute.

BEEF TAJINE WITH PRUNES

Serves 6–8

45 ml (3 T) olive or sunflower oil

1 large onion, chopped

2 garlic cloves, crushed

1 kg (2½ lb) stewing beef, cut into large portions

50 ml (3 T) chopped parsley

5 ml (1 t) ground cinnamon

5 ml (1 t) ground cumin

3 ml (½ t) ground ginger

10 ml (2 t) freshly ground black pepper

3 ml (½ t) saffron or 5 ml (1 t) turmeric

750 ml (3 cups) water

250 g (9 oz) prunes, halved and stoned

15 ml (1 T) clear honey

salt to taste

toasted sesame seeds

chopped almonds

1 In a large saucepan, heat the oil and stir in the onions, garlic, beef, parsley and spices. Cook until the meat is browned all over.

2 Stir in the water and simmer, covered, for about 1½ hours until the meat is tender.

3 Add the prunes, honey and salt. Cover again and simmer for a further 30 minutes.

4 Serve on couscous (*see* recipe on page 128) and garnish with sesame seeds and almonds.

VEGETABLE STEW

Serves 6–8
60 ml (4 T) olive or sunflower oil
2 onions, chopped
2 garlic cloves, crushed
10 ml (2 t) ground ginger
3 ml (½ t) saffron or 5 ml (1 t) turmeric
250 g (9 oz) each of vegetables in season,
e.g. potatoes, carrots, courgettes, cabbage
or green brinjal, cut into large pieces
water
salt and pepper

TOPPING
1 onion, chopped
15 ml (1 T) olive oil
45 ml (3 T) sultanas
2 ml (½ t) cumin
salt and pepper to taste

1 Heat oil, add onions, garlic, ginger and saffron or turmeric and sauté until tender.
2 Add vegetables. Place in a large saucepan with enough water to cover. Season. Cook 20 minutes.
4 TOPPING: Fry the onion in olive oil until transparent. Add the sultanas, cumin, salt and pepper.
5 Spoon vegetables onto couscous (*see* recipe this page). If preferred, cooked meat or chicken can be placed first. Top with onion and fruit mixture.

> Couscous is Morocco's staple food. It is made from semolina that has been coarsely ground, moistened and rolled in flour.

COUSCOUS

Serves 6–8
500 g (18 oz) couscous
60 ml (4 T) *smen/ghee* or melted butter
250 ml (1 cup) boiling water

1 Gently rub the *smen/ghee* or melted butter into the couscous (this helps to separate the grains).
2 Pour over the boiling water, stir well and leave for 10 minutes. Fork through the couscous to make sure the grains separate.
3 Put into a steamer or colander over a pot of gently cooking meat or vegetables and cook, uncovered, for 20 minutes.
4 Fork through the couscous again to separate the grains, turn on to a warm serving dish, dot with butter, and form into a mound with a large well in the centre into which to ladle the meat and/or vegetables.

The mellow flavour of preserved lemons and the pink-brown Moroccan olives give this dish its unique character.

TAJINE DE POULET MQUALLI

CHICKEN TAJINE WITH OLIVES AND PRESERVED LEMONS

SERVES 4

45 ml (3 T) olive oil

1 onion, chopped

3 garlic cloves, crushed

salt and pepper to taste

3 ml (½ t) ground ginger

8 ml (1½ t) ground cinnamon

large pinch of saffron threads or

3 ml (½ t) ground saffron

1,5 kg (3½ lb) chicken

700 ml (2½ cups) chicken stock or water

100 g (4 oz)/125 ml (½ cup) green-brown Moroccan olives, drained, or green and black olives, drained

1 preserved lemon, peeled, rinsed and chopped

1 bunch coriander leaves, finely chopped

1 Heat the oil and fry the onions until golden.

2 Crush together the garlic, salt, pepper, ginger, cinnamon and saffron. Stir into the onions, cook until fragrant and spread over the chicken.

3 Place chicken in a heavy saucepan or oven-proof casserole. Add the stock or water and heat until boiling. Reduce the heat, cover and simmer for 1½ hours, turning the chicken 2 to 3 times.

4 Add the olives, preserved lemon and herbs. Cover again and cook for 15 minutes. Check the seasoning, transfer the chicken to a serving dish and keep warm. Cut into portions if prefered.

5 Reduce the cooking juices to a rich sauce, skim off excess fat and pour the sauce over the chicken. Serve with couscous (*see* page 128).

PRESERVED LEMONS

30 ml (2 T) coarse salt

12 plump juicy lemons, preferably thin-skinned

1 Put 10 ml (2 t) coarse salt in a preserving jar.

2 Using a sharp knife and working on a plate, slice the lemons lengthways but not right through – leave the pieces joined at the bottom.

3 Remove any pips, pack 15 ml (1 T) coarse salt into the cuts, close the lemons and pack them into the jar. Pack the jar tightly.

4 Squeeze another lemon, pour the juice over the fruit, sprinkle with the remaining coarse salt and top up with boiling water to cover the fruit.

5 Close the jar tightly and keep in a warm place for 3 to 4 weeks. A white film might appear on top of the lemons – this is normal and harmless.

VARIATION: This also works well with limes. If prefered, 1 stick cinnamon, 3 whole cloves, 6 crushed coriander seeds, 3 black peppercorns and 1 bay leaf can be layered with the lemons.

Preserved lemons play a major role in Moroccan cooking, and make a novel addition to non-Moroccan dishes. Thin-skinned lemons will yield the most juice. Once the jar has been opened, pour in a little olive oil to cover the surface and the lemons will keep for up to a year.

1 Combine the milk, cornflour and sugar. Heat until boiling, reduce the heat and simmer, stirring until thick.

2 Cut the phyllo pastry into large circles. Place alternate layers of phyllo pastry sheets and milk sauce on a round baking tray, top with nuts and bake for about 20 minutes in the oven at 180 °C (350 °F/gas 4) until golden.

HUMMOUS

SERVES 4–6

250 ml (1 cup) chickpeas

water

250 g (9 oz) sesame seeds

1 garlic clove, crushed

lemon juice to taste

15 ml (1 T) olive oil

salt

1 Soak the chickpeas overnight in water. Drain.

2 Put fresh water into a saucepan, add the chickpeas and cook until almost tender. Drain. Add sesame seeds and garlic.

3 In a blender or pestle and mortar, blend with as much chickpea water as needed into a thick purée. Add lemon juice, salt and pepper to taste.

5 TO SERVE: Place the hummous in a ceramic bowl, make a hollow in the middle and pour in a little olive oil.

Desserts are not common in African cuisine. A meal is usually rounded off with fresh fruit. Pastilla, with a milky sauce, is one of the few pastry desserts served in Morocco.

PASTILLA WITH MILK

SERVES 6–8

500 ml (2 cups) milk

30 ml (2 T) cornflour

30 ml (2 T) sugar

5–6 sheets phyllo pastry

250 ml (1 cup) chopped mixed nuts

TABOULEH

SERVES 4–6

250 ml (1 cup) finely ground bulgur (cracked wheat)

125 ml (½ cup) parsley, finely chopped

125 ml (½ cup) mint leaves, finely chopped

2 firm tomatoes, peeled and diced

4 spring onions, finely chopped

salt and pepper

5 ml (1 t) *soemak* (Arabic spice)

45 ml (3 T) olive oil

45 ml (3 T) lemon juice

1 Soak the bulgur in water for 2 to 3 hours. Drain well.

2 Mix the parsley and mint with the tomatoes and onions.

3 Mix remaining ingredients. Pour over salad and toss well. Serve as part of the *mezes*.

BABAGHANUSH

SERVES 4–6

1 kg (2½ lb) brinjals

125 ml (½ cup) sesame oil

125 ml (½ cup) yoghurt

30 ml (2 T) chopped parsley

1 garlic clove, crushed

30 ml (2 T) lemon juice

30 ml (2 T) olive oil

½ cucumber to garnish

salt and black pepper

1 Bake or roast the brinjals in their skin at 180 °C (350 °F/gas 4) for about 1 hour until they are soft, and immerse immediately in cold water with lemon juice to preserve the colour. Cool, then peel, drain the juice and mash until smooth.

2 Add the rest of the ingredients and mix well. Place the mixture in a ceramic dish and garnish with cucumber slices.

> This dish is served as part of the *mezes*.
> Mezes are made up of a number of small dishes used as a first course.

RIGHT, CLOCKWISE FROM TOP LEFT *Tabouleh, Babaghanush, Hummous and Shanhlish (feta cheese with cumin and cayene pepper)*

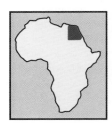

EGYPT

The metropolis of the universe, the garden of the world, the anthill of the human species, the throne of royalty, a city embellished with castles and palaces, its horizon decorated with monasteries and with schools, and lit by the moons and stars of education. So said one Bin Khaldun, a great medieval Arab historian, about Cairo.

Cairo, also dubbed the 'Mother of the World', is said to be the largest city in Africa, and has a long and rich history. This last outpost of the African continent also completes the journey through Africa, from the Cape to Cairo.

Egypt lies on the northeastern point of Africa, stretching to the Mount Sinai region across the Suez Canal. The great Nile River flows from the south to the Mediterranean, and it is the fertile valleys of this river that sheltered one of the earliest known civilisations. Along with those of Mesopotamia, the Indus valley and China, it was one of the oldest civilisations, stretching back as far as 6 000 years to the time of the pharaohs. The pyramids and the Sphinx, Byzantine Coptic churches and Roman ruins attract travellers from all over the world.

Egypt's population of around 64 million is generally mixed, but basically of Mediterranean stock, and the national languages are Arabic, French and English.

Every part of Africa has some green leaf that is considered a delicacy. In South Africa it is the *morogo*, in Kenya *sukuma wiki*, Malawi and Zimbabwe have *rape*, Mozambique has *matapa*, Zambians love *ifisyasi* and *kalembula*, and Egypt's wonder is *moloukia*.

The food in Egypt is a combination of Arabic and Mediterranean, with *mezes*, *moussaka* and *canneloni* forming part of the local cuisine.

However, like every country, Egyptians have their authentic dishes, such as *tamia*, *foul* and *kochari*. Pigeons are also a local delicacy and, feathered and gutted while you wait, they are sold in most street markets. You will probably be advised to buy a pair – lest you leave the companion lonely and sad.

The street café is the heart of Egyptian street life, but like much of Africa, it is a largely male preserve. The coffeehouses provide a pleasant atmosphere for patrons to relax over a cup of sweet Egyptian tea or Arabic coffee while smoking *shiisha*, or a water pipe.

LEFT *Ancient Egyptian bas relief.*
ABOVE *An Egyptian girl weaving a carpet.*
OPPOSITE *A 'desert taxi' and its proud owner.*

BAMIA SAUCE

OKRA SAUCE

SERVES 4–6

60 ml (4 T) oil

2 onions, chopped

500 g (18 oz) minced beef

500 ml (2 cups) tomato juice

1 kg (2½ lb) okra, cleaned and sliced

5 garlic cloves, crushed

3 ml (½ t) ground coriander

salt to taste

1 Heat 30 ml (2 T) of the oil and fry the onions until golden. Add the minced beef and brown.

2 Add tomato juice. Simmer for 10 minutes.

3 Reduce heat, add okra and stir until mixed.

4 In another pan, heat rest of oil and fry garlic and coriander. Add salt. Toss into okra and simmer for 7 minutes. Serve with rice or pita bread.

FETAH

SERVES 4–6

1 litre (4 cups) water

2 onions, chopped

5 cardamom seeds

salt and pepper to taste

1 kg (2½ lb) lamb, cut into cubes

6 slices white bread

15 ml (3 t) oil

10 garlic cloves, crushed

30 ml (2 T) vinegar

500 ml (2 cups) cooked rice

1 In a large saucepan, bring the water to the boil and then add the onions, cardamom seeds, salt and pepper. Add the lamb and cook for about 45 minutes until tender.

2 Remove the meat from the broth and keep warm. Discard the cardamom seeds and mash the onion until smooth.

3 Cut the bread into small squares and place it in a serving dish.

4 Heat the oil, add the garlic and fry until pale gold. Add vinegar and boil for 3 to 5 minutes. Pour into the broth and simmer for 5 minutes.

5 TO SERVE: Moisten the bread with some of the broth and cover it with a thick layer of rice. Moisten the rice with the remaining soup. Arrange the meat around the rice in a ring.

KEBABS

SERVES 4–6

KOFTAS

500 g (18 oz) minced meat

1 small onion, finely chopped

25 ml (2 T) mixed fresh herbs, such as thyme, basil, parsley and oregano, finely chopped

salt and pepper to taste

250 ml (1 cup) fresh breadcrumbs

500 g (18 oz) lamb cubes

2 large onions, cut into large chunks

2 firm, large tomatoes, cut into wedges

1 KOFTAS: Mix the minced meat, onion, herbs, seasoning and crumbs. Form into small balls.

2 Thread the *koftas*, lamb cubes, onions and tomatoes on skewers. Grill over white-hot charcoal until done. Serve with pita bread.

TURKEY WITH RICE AND KHALTA

SERVES 6–8

1 turkey of 1–1,5 kg (2½–3½ lb)

45 ml (3 T) flour

15 ml (1 T) mustard

60 ml (4 T) sugar

125 g (4½ oz)/125 ml (½ cup) butter

250 ml (1 cup) Egyptian rice

1 chicken stock cube, dissolved in:

250 ml (1 cup) hot water

125 ml (½ cup) flaked almonds

125 ml (½ cup) each raisins and sultanas

1 Rub turkey with flour, leave to stand, then rinse with water. Rub with mustard. Roast at 180° C (350 °F/ gas 4) for 2 to 3 hours, depending on the size of the turkey.

2 Melt the sugar and butter together until brown.

3 Add the rice and stir to coat. Add the stock and heat until boiling. Lower heat and simmer for 20 minutes or until the rice is cooked.

4 Spoon the rice on to a large platter and place the turkey on top. Scatter the nuts, raisins and sultanas on the rice.

> Egyptian rice has shorter grains than American rice. For the latter, use 2 cups of water to 1 cup of rice.

2 In another pan, fry the onions in the oil until rich brown. Remove with a slotted spoon.
3 Strain the oil in which the onions were fried into the lentil mixture and cook for 10 minutes, stirring lightly to prevent sticking. Season.
4 Serve topped with heated Mediterranean tomato mix and fried onions.

KUBEEBA

SERVES 4

500 g (18 oz) bulgur

500 g (18 oz) minced beef

1 onion, grated

salt and pepper to taste

oil for deep-frying

FILLING

500 g (18 oz) minced beef

1 garlic clove, crushed

1 onion, finely chopped

pinch each of of cumin, coriander

and paprika

salt and pepper to taste

1 Soak the bulgur for 20 minutes. Drain and mix with the mince, onion and seasoning.
2 FILLING: Sauté the minced beef, garlic, onion, spices, salt and pepper for 20 minutes until cooked.

3 With wet hands, take a small piece of the bulgur-and-mince mixture and place it in the palm of your hand. With the index finger of the other hand, make a hole in the *kubeeba* and rotate, half closing the palm until it becomes very thin. Half-fill with filling and a small dot of butter. Moisten the hand again and close the *kubeeba* to form a round or egg-shaped ball.
4 Heat the oil and deep-fry the kubeeba on all sides until brown, or place in a greased oven tin, brush the top with cooking oil and roast in a pre-heated oven at 180 °C (350 °F/gas 4) until brown all over.

> *Kubeeba* – oval-shaped meatballs with a minced-meat filling – are served as snacks or starters. Bulgur (crushed wheat) is available from health shops, some supermarkets and delicatessens.

> *Kochari* is a very popular dish, enjoyed especially during the no-meat times.

KOCHARI

SERVES 4

200 g (7 oz)/250 ml (1 cup) brown lentils

250 ml (1 cup) rice

125 ml (½ cup) macaroni

2 onions, chopped

60 ml (4 T) oil

salt and pepper to taste

1 can (410g/14 oz) Mediterranean tomato mix

1 Cook the lentils, rice and macaroni separately according to the directions on the packets. Place these three ingredients together in a pot.

MOLOUKIA

Serves 4

1 bunch moloukia or spinach, finely chopped

250 ml (1 cup) chicken or meat stock

2 garlic cloves, crushed

3 ml (½ t) ground coriander

60 g (2½ oz)/62,5 ml (¼ cup) butter or ghee, melted

1 Add the moloukia to chicken or meat stock and boil for 10 minutes.

2 Heat the melted butter or ghee, add garlic and coriander and sauté. Add to the moloukia. Serve with bread or rice and fried chicken or meat.

YOGHURT ZABADIE BELKHEIAR

YOGHURT WITH CUCUMBER

Serves 4

175 ml (½ cup) natural yoghurt

1 cucumber, cut into small pieces

1 green pepper, finely chopped

salt to taste

1 Mix all the ingredients together.

2 Serve as a salad.

LISAN ASFOUR

'TONGUE OF BIRD'

Serves 4

50 ml (¼ cup) water

250 ml (1 cup) rice pasta

500 g (18 oz) meat cubes or mince

1 onion, chopped

1 garlic clove, crushed

1 green pepper, chopped

3 ml (½ t) coriander

3 ml (½ t) cumin

2 tomatoes, sliced

1 Heat the water to boiling point in a saucepan. Boil the rice pasta and meat with the onion, –garlic, green pepper and spices.

2 Place the mixture in an oven-proof dish. Bake in a moderate oven (180 °C/350 °F/gas 4) for 20 minutes

3 Top with the tomato slices and serve with fried chicken.

> Rice pasta, which is sold in most supermarkets, is the main ingredient of this dish. Because of the size and shape of the pasta, it is referred to as 'tongue of bird'.

RIGHT *Moloukia and Lisam Asfour.*

UMA' ALI

SERVES 4–6
500 g (18 oz) phyllo pastry
250 ml (1 cup) mixed nuts
15 ml (1 T) desiccated coconut
15 ml (1 T) cream
500 ml (2 cups) milk sweetened with:
62,5 ml (¼ cup) sugar
125 ml (½ cup) raisins

1 Preheat the oven to 200 °C (400 °F/gas 6).
2 Bake 1 to 2 sheets of pastry at a timefor 2 to 3 minutes until dry and crisp. Crush with your fingers and place in a lightly greased oven dish.
2 Mix the nuts, raisins and coconut. Scatter this mixture on top of the crushed pastry.
3 Warm the sweetened milk and pour over the dessert. Dab with butter or cream and place in moderately hot oven (200 °C/400 °F/gas 6) until the top is browned.

FOUL

SERVES 4–6
250 ml (1 cup) dry broad beans
250 ml (1 cup) red lentils
1 garlic clove, crushed
45 ml (3 T) oil
2 tomatoes, chopped
2 onions, chopped

1 Soak the beans overnight in water. Retain the water and cook until soft.
2 Add the red lentils and garlic.
3 Heat the oil in a pan and fry the tomatoes and onions together. Mix with the beans and lentils. Serve hot or cold.

KICHK

MILKY COLD SAUCE

SERVES 4
60 g (2 oz)/125 ml (½ cup) flour
salt and pepper to taste
500 ml (2 cups) tinned chicken soup
250 ml (1 cup) milk
1 onion, sliced
15 ml (1 T) butter

1 Mix the flour and seasoning. Add the chicken soup to the milk and pour over the flour, stirring to blend.
2 Place over a low heat and cook, stirring constantly until slightly thickened. Place in a shallow dish to cool.
3 Fry the onion in the butter until brown. Drain and allow to cool, then place the onion over the kichk. Serve cold.
VARIATION: For a green sauce, add 60 ml (4 T) chopped fresh coriander to the chicken soup and milk mixture.

> *Kichk* is served on its own or as part of the mezes.

This is a popular and economical Egyptian dish, served at breakfast.

TAMIA

MAKES 4–6

250 ml (1 cup) chickpeas or dry beans

15 ml (1 T) coriander leaves, chopped

15 ml (1 T) dill, chopped

15 ml (1 T) parsley, chopped

salt and pepper

3 ml (½ t) ground coriander

3 ml (½ t) ground cumin

4 spring onions, chopped

pinch of bicarbonate of soda

oil for deep frying

1 Soak the chickpeas or dry beans overnight and crush.

2 Mix the chickpeas or dry beans with the coriander, dill and parsley. Season with salt, pepper, ground coriander and cumin.

3 Add spring onion and a pinch of bicarbonate of soda. Form into patties and deep-fry in hot oil. Serve with foul.

VARIATION: To prepare *bisar,* a dish served with bread, pickles or salad, add more greens to the ingredients.

THE ABC OF AFRICAN INGREDIENTS

AGUSHI (EGUSI)

Ground melon seed, widely used in West African cooking to add a creamy texture and nutty flavour to dishes. Ground almonds can be used as a substitute.

AMADUMBE 'MADUMBIS'

A favourite of the Zulu people in Natal. These tubers have a very course, rough skin. Amadumbes are simply boiled in their skin until soft, peeled and then sliced or cut into wedges. They are eaten on their own as a snack or served as a side dish. Some supermarkets sell them.

BAOBAB FRUIT

Baobab fruit is round and quite hard, and the seeds, strings and powder inside quite acidic. The powder is also used in place of cream of tartar.

BRINJAL (AUBERGINE, EGGPLANT)

An elongated or rounded fruit with a shiny purple skin. This white variety is often used in African and Mediterranean dishes.

CARDAMOM

A member of the ginger family; these seeds are also known as 'the seed of Paradise'. It is available ground or whole and is used to flavour soups, eggs, noodles, custards, breyanis, puddings and cakes.

CASSAVA (MANDIOCA)

A tropical vegetable with tuberous roots, a brown skin and starchy flesh, similar to sweet potatoes. Cassava is commonly used in West and East African dishes. The peel is slit down to the flesh with a sharp knife, and then pulled away like a banana peel. The tuber is sliced lengthways to remove the core, which resembles thick string. Plain boiled cassava may replace potatoes in any meal. Dried and ground, it makes cassava flour and gari.

CHILLIES

Fresh or dried chillies are widely used in African cookery. Dried, powdered chillies are known as cayenne pepper. Green chillies have more flavour and are juicier, while red chillies are hotter and must be used sparingly.

CLOVES

Zanzibar used to be the sole exporter of this precious spice. Now it is grown in a number of other countries. Cloves – the unopened buds of the myrtaceous tree – are picked when they turn red and are then sun dried. Ground cloves are stronger than whole ones. They are used to flavour both savoury and sweet dishes.

COCONUT MILK

Widely used in East African cooking. A fresh coconut is cut or broken in half. The flesh is shredded or grated, and mixed with cold water. After a few minutes it is placed in a conical basket or colander and squeezed to produce the milk. Coconut milk can also be made by simmering desiccated coconut in water and then rubbing it through a sieve to extract the fluid.

COURGETTE (BABY MARROW, ZUCCHINI)

This vegetable, a member of the marrow family, is now used all over Africa. It has a shiny skin and firm watery flesh, and is best eaten when young.

COUSCOUS

The staple food in African countries such as Morocco, Tunisia and Algeria. It is semolina that has been coarsely ground, moistened and rolled in flour.

CUMIN

An aromatic plant with long spindle-shaped seeds that are used as a condiment and a flavouring. It has a hot, piquant and slightly bitter taste.

DHANIA

Fresh coriander leaves which are used to garnish curries or add flavour to savoury dishes and salads. It is also available in powdered form.

DRIED MEAT

This is especially popular in Venda and Zimbabwe. Red meat is sliced into strips and sun dried. It can be eaten on its own when dry or cooked in a ground nut sauce. In South Africa it is generally known as *biltong*; among the Shona it is known as *chumukuyu*, and among the Zulus as *umqweyiba* .

FUFU

Fufu is prepared from boiled cassava (*see* cassava), which is pounded to a pulp and then puréed until it is free of lumps, after which it is made into balls.

GARI

Dried, ground cassava (*see* cassava). Gari can be replaced with cooked *phutu*.

GROUND NUTS

Ground and sifted peanuts are widely used in southern African as well as west African cooking.

GROUNDNUT PASTE

This paste of ground peanuts and water is especially popular in West Africa as an ingredient of sauces and light soups. Use peanut butter as substitute.

KENKEY

This is a very popular Ghanaian dish made from fermented maize-meal (*see* maize-meal).

MAIZE-MEAL

Ground and sometimes refined maize. Cooked into a porridge, it is a staple food of most of Africa. In Malawi it is called *nsima*, in Kenya it is known as *ugali*, and in Zimbabwe and Malawi it is called *sadza*.

MAIZE-RICE

Rice-shaped grain made from maize, popular in South African traditional cooking. It is sometimes mixed into sour porridge (*ting*).

MINT

A fresh-tasting herb with a strong flavour. In North and West Africa it is used to flavour tea.

MOPANE WORMS

Mopane worms are eaten mostly in southern Africa, and are a delicacy among the Venda, Tsonga and Pedi people. The worms fall off the mopane tree, after which they are named. Mopane worms are a rich source of protein. They are usually dried and kept for up to a year and fried in fat or cooked in a ground nut stew or tomato and onion sauce. Mopane worms are known as *mashonzha* in Venda, as *phane* in Botswana, and as *madora* or *amacimbi* in Zimbabwe.

MOROGO

Morogo is a collective term for various leaves, some of them wild. *Morogo* is typical of South Africa and can be substituted with spinach. The different African countries have their own national green leaves, e.g. *moloukia* in Egypt, *matapa* in Malawi, *cacani* in Mozambique, *sukuma wiki* or *muchicha* in Kenya, and *rape* in Zambia and Zimbabwe.

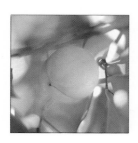

NUTMEG

Nutmeg comes from an evergreen tree. It can be freshly grated just before using or bought ground. The dry membrane that surrounds the seed is mace.

OKRA (OKRO, THERERE)

Also referred to a ladies' fingers, okra is widely used in African cooking. When purchasing okra, avoid the large variety, choose small firm ones.

PALM OIL

Palm oil is extracted from palm nuts which are boiled and pounded into pulp. Palm oil prepared at home is thick and red or yellowish in colour.

PEPPER

Black pepper is derived from berries that are picked just before they ripen. Ripe berries are sun dried and ground to form white pepper.

PLANTAINS

Family of the banana. Inedible when raw, but once cooked, boiled, fried, roasted or baked they have a great flavour. Used mostly in West and East Africa.

SAFFRON

A rare and expensive spice. It is used to tint and flavour savoury dishes into a yellow colour. This spice is made from the stamens of the wild crocus.

SAMP

Maize kernels that heve been stamped and broken but not ground as fine as maize-rice or maize-meal. It is a Xhosa staple food, but it is also eaten in most of South Africa.

SMEN (GHEE)

Smen or *ghee* is clarified fat, which is commonly used in North African cooking. It is also a very popular ingredient in Indian cooking. The best *smen* is made from butter.

SWEET POTATOES

These are usually reddish brown skinned, although in other parts of the continent you might find them with white skins. They can be boiled in their jacket, peeled and cooked and mashed, sliced and deep fried to make chips or oven baked.

TAMBI

Tambi is a type of egg noodle that looks like tiny ribbons. It is a favourite of Zanzibar, where it is cooked and mixed with sugar and ground cardamom.

TING

Sour or fermented porridge (Botswana).

TURMERIC (BORRIE)

Turmeric, a member of the ginger family, comes from a perennial tropical plant. The root is dried and ground and used to colour curries and rice.

WARKA

North African equivalent of phyllo pastry.

YAM

The yam is a tuber of a climbing plant. These tubers mature in the dry season and look like enormous rough potatoes. They may be egg shaped, elongated or flattened, and come in all sizes. The flesh is either yellow or white and can be eaten boiled, roasted, baked, mashed or made into chips. Sweet potatoes may be substituted for yams.

WHOLE PEPPERS

Whole peppers are used in most of Africa especially North Africa with its Mediterranean influence. These peppers can now be found in a variety of exotic colours, such as black, white and yellow. Also known as capsicums, the flavours vary according to varieties, they can be sweet, fiery, mild or hot.

INDEX